On the F

By the same Author:

Look and Listen—Young People's Addresses for Parade Services and Family Services—using Visual Aids. (Chester House Publications).
Look and Listen Through the Year—Children's Addresses for Family Services, Parade Services and other occasions—using Visual Aids. (The Saint Andrew Press).
Twentieth Century Christians—Twelve Mini-Biographies. (The Saint Andrew Press)

On the Right Track

Contemporary Christians in Sport

John D Searle

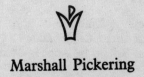

Marshall Pickering

Marshall Morgan and Scott
Marshall Pickering
3 Beggarwood Lane, Basingstoke,
Hants RG23 7LP, UK

British Library CIP Data
Searle, John D.
   On the right track: contemporary
   Christians in sport.
   1. Christian biography
   I. Title
   209'.2'2   BR1700.2

ISBN 0–551–01424–5

Text Phototypeset in Linotron Plantin 10 on 11 point
by Input Typesetting Ltd., London SW19 8DR
Printed in Great Britain by Anchor Brendon Ltd,
Tiptree, Essex.

CONTENTS

'Surely you know that many runners take part in a race, but only one of them wins the prize. Run, then, in such a way as to win the prize. Every athlete in training submits to strict discipline, in order to be crowned with a wreath that will not last; but we do it for one that will last for ever. That is why I run straight for the finishing-line; that is why I am like a boxer who does not waste his punches. I harden my body with blows and bring it under complete control to keep myself from being disqualified after having called others to the contest.'

1 Corinthians 9 vv. 24–27: Good News Bible.

Foreword

by John Motson, BBC Television *Match of the Day* Commentator

Anybody who doubts the relevance of Christianity to the colourful world of professional entertainment would have been interested, if not moved, by a recent conversation between singer Cliff Richard and a top football club manager.

They met at a dinner in Hertfordshire organised by the North London branch of a rapidly growing organisation called 'Christians in Sport'.

Cliff's own faith has been publicly aired many times, and has never failed to stand the test. But his gift for expressing privately his deep convictions, and the carefully considered reasons behind them, is something else.

Having spent the last twenty years or more in the blistering, electric world of popular music, he knows what it takes to be a Christian in a difficult environment. And he knows that professional sport, and English soccer in particular, is not so far removed from rock and roll when it comes to the peculiar demands made on prize performers.

Hence he was able to relate quickly to the probing questions of the football manager, and to answer them with a direct simplicity which was almost stunning. Their conversation was one of many between committed Christians and inquiring sports people in an era when many stars are wondering just what else lies beyond the short term adulation they may receive.

Such a theme was what John Searle had in mind when

he approached the considerable task of putting on paper the Christian experience of a selected number of sportsmen and women. Their route to success in their own sphere may have been different, as indeed was their route to a firm belief in God, but they have in common the enviable combination of sporting prowess and religious conviction.

Two things in particular struck me when I read the manuscript. The first was a confirmation that God knows no barriers to His outreach. Secondly, the subjects that John Searle has studied share two important things—an unshakeable belief in God and a controlled competitiveness which enables them to continue to pursue their sporting ambition without allowing it to weaken their faith.

It would be pointless of me to say any more when the proof of the argument lies in the reading ahead. I am sure those who have a Christian belief will find it strengthened by the experience of those whose lives are opened up here, and I hope those who may still be looking for the true meaning in life might be led closer to God by the sincerity which shines through the pages which follow.

John Motson
St Albans
1986.

Introduction

The aim of this book is to tell the stories of a number of Christians who have made a name in the contemporary world of sport.

Like my previous book. *Twentieth Century Christians*, I hope that these brief studies will be of interest both to the general reader—of all ages—and to those responsible for Christian education and apologetic in the broadest sense (R.E., school assemblies, talks to church groups, and so on).

In past years there have been a number of notable British sportsmen who have been Christians, for example C T Studd—Cambridge University and England cricketer, Billy Liddell—Liverpool and Scotland footballer, and Eric Liddell—winner of the 400 metres in the 1924 Olympic Games. Here, however, I have confined myself to *contemporary* sports people, and not all are of British origin. The larger number of sports*men* featured here reflects the proportion of men and women taking part in sport rather than any male chauvinism!

It is hoped that the discovery that there are top-class sports people who are also committed Christians will help to correct the widespread misapprehension that Christianity is merely a crutch for the feeble. In an age when sports people enjoy the adulation of thousands of fans, they are in a unique position to influence others for Christ. As the American *Guideposts* magazine put it, 'Hero worship can be dangerous both for the worshipper *and* the hero, but if hero worship can be turned away from the sports personality to the Person, then both will benefit.'

I am very grateful to those featured here who have spared their time to talk or write to me. I am also grateful to the authors and publishers who have allowed me to use material found in their publications; these are listed at the end of each chapter under the heading *For Further Reading*.

I wish to thank several others: Mr John Motson for writing a Foreword; my father-in-law, the Revd Dr C Leslie Mitton, and Mr Stuart J Weir, Secretary of 'Christians in Sport', for reading these chapters and offering many helpful sugestions; and to Mrs Ann Grice and Mrs Wendy Forman for typing the manuscript. I am also grateful to my wife, Joan, for her patience while I have worked on this book on my 'day-off'!

John D Searle
Goodrington: October 1985.

1: Bat and Crosier

David Sheppard: Cricketer and Bishop

Born 6 March 1929

At the age of eight, David Sheppard played in his first proper cricket match. Batting for the Slinfold Colts against a Veterans' XI, he made 23 runs. Cricket now became the absorbing interest in his life and school holidays included many days spent as a spectator at the Sussex County ground at Hove, with the added excitement of a day or two at Lord's or the Oval to see a Test Match. When he was ten, David won a place in the 1st XI at his preparatory school; he batted last but took several wickets. Until he was sixteen, he was small for his age and not strong enough to be a dominant batsman. However, at seventeen, he was selected for the 1st XI at Sherborne School. Although in each of his first two matches he was out for 0, gradually, the runs came, and one of his masters, Micky Walford, a Somerset player, said to him, 'You ought to be a first-class cricketer'. The idea had never entered David's head before, but from that day he was determined to play in first-class cricket.

In 1946, David played twice for Young Sussex against Young Yorkshire and made 50 in each match. That September he received a letter from Billy Griffith, the Sussex captain and secretary, congratulating him and inviting him to practise at the nets with the county players the following April. The letter was treasured during the Winter, and David could hardly believe it when, on the first day of practice, he found himself at the nets with players whose exploits he had followed for many years. Back at school for his last term, David reaped the benefit of this net practice, making 786 runs in ten completed

11

innings. That summer, he played at Lord's for the first time, in a two-day game, Southern Schools v. the Rest.

David was eighteen when he played his first county match for Sussex against Leicestershire, at Hastings. He was out first ball in the first innings and did only a little better in the second innings, being 0 not out at the tea interval on the third day. As they returned to play, the Leicestershire captain said, 'There'll be a run for you on the off-side if you want it'. All the fielders moved back so that David could push an easy single; he got one more run without help before being caught. Against Warwickshire he made 15 and 0, and against Essex had one good drive through the covers for 4. It was not an outstanding debut, but to the discerning eye, the potential of this young batsman was evident.

The next two years were spent in the Army doing National Service. Whenever possible, David played cricket, mostly club cricket or for the Sussex 2nd XI. In the last match of the 1948 season, he made his first century in county cricket—157 not out against Kent 2nd XI. This gave him confidence and resulted in improved batting performances. In June 1949, he made his first 50 for the Sussex 1st XI, playing against Oxford University, but after a series of dropped catches, he was back in the 2nd XI. He then made 100 against Essex 2nd XI and was brought back into the 1st XI for their next match against Glamorgan. After three hours, he had only made 43 against tight, defensive bowling. George Cox at the other end came up the wicket and challenged David, 'You say you can hit the ball through the covers. Well, put your leg up the wicket and hit the ball.' He finished the day at 199 and, after reaching 204 the next morning, he was awarded his Sussex cap. With renewed confidence, he went on to score two more centuries before going up to Cambridge University.

In addition to playing cricket, David planned to read History and Law at Cambridge! Life was full, but there was always time for endless debate on politics and religion. Christian ideas of morality and worship had been impressed on David as a boy and he held high ideals as a teenager. He was confirmed when he was thirteen and had tried to attend Church regularly. Faced, in the Army, with men of all beliefs and none, he had become increasingly dissatisfied with himself and with religion. God seemed remote and prayer futile; it was a case of struggling on in the hope of gaining a deeper faith as time went by. The turning point in his life came when John Collins, a student at Ridley Hall, Cambridge, subsequently vicar of Holy Trinity Church, Brompton Road, London, played David at squash and afterwards they had a cup of tea together. There was a mission taking place at the university and John invited David to go along with him to Great St Mary's Church. The speaker was a blunt and aggressive preacher from America, Dr Donald Barnhouse. He pointed out that being a faithful church member did not automatically make a person right with God, declaring that it is not by one's own efforts but only by the grace of Jesus Christ that anyone can be accepted and forgiven by God.

After the meeting, John invited David back to his room and, as they talked, David sensed that his friend had something sadly missing in his own life. John helped him to see that if you sincerely ask Christ to come into your life, life will never be quite the same again. Later David walked back to his rooms in Trinity Hall. In his autobiography, *Parsons Pitch*, David recalls that momentous evening—'I knew that it was more important than anything else in the world that I should become right with God. I knelt in my bedroom and, praying in my own words, I asked Christ to come into my life to forgive me and to be my Friend and Master. Then I prayed, "Lord, I don't know where this is going to take me but I'm willing to go with You—please make me willing." '

'It was as if a jumble of loose threads suddenly fitted into place. It had all happened to me very suddenly in one sense, but there had been years of Christian background which helped me to understand what it was all about.'

There was no dramatic change in his feelings or actions

13

after he had made his act of commitment, but as he met other enthusiastic young Christians, David gradually grew in faith. He gained considerable help as they discussed problems of belief and practice. In particular, he questioned whether it was right for him to spend so much time playing cricket. He came to the conclusion that if Christ wants his followers fully involved in the world of men, then it *was* right for him to give at least some years of his life to the game.

'I have often been asked if religion and cricket can mix. . . . I believe that health, strength, quickness of eye, all come from God. Success comes from God—and so too can failure. If I say my prayers faithfully, this is no guarantee that I shall make a hundred next time I go in to bat. I may make a duck or hundred to the glory of God—by the way I accept success or failure.'

Although a Freshman and only twenty, David went straight into the University 1st XI and made 130 in their opening match—against his own county, Sussex!

A fine score of 227 against the West Indies led to a Test Trial match, in which he scored 4 out of his team's grand total of 27! His big chance came later in the 1950 season. Coming in at the tea interval during a match against Surrey, David found a telegram on his dressing-room locker. Cyril Washbrook was injured and David had been selected to take his place for England against the West Indies.

It was a schoolboy's dream come true when David went in at number three to join the legendary Len Hutton. He reached 11 and was beginning to settle down when over the loudspeakers came the announcement of the birth of Princess Anne. A large crowd of West Indians started chanting, 'Let's have a wicket for the Princess'. Ramadhin bowled a long teasing half volley and David was the Princess' birthday wicket!

David had played well enough to be selected to join Freddie Brown's team to tour Australia in 1950–51. Although he did not make many runs, he served his apprenticeship playing at this, the highest competitive level. There were other lessons learned, too. It was not easy living up to his new-found faith away from home and constantly on the move. He discovered the importance of Christian friends. John Dewes, a fellow Cambridge undergraduate, was someone with whom he could discuss his doubts, read the Bible and pray while on tour. They were invited to speak at several informal groups of young people, a challenge which helped David's own faith to grow deeper. Five months in Australia were followed by a hurried month's tour of New Zealand, which gave him more valuable experience.

In his second year, David was elected Secretary for the University Cricket Club, and the following year he became Captain. He was surprised at his election as he had assumed that the choice would fall on Peter May, his contemporary at Cambridge, who had captained the English Schools side when they were both eighteen. It was in a match against Worcestershire that he made his highest score in first-class cricket. With five hours left to play, the University needed 373 to win. Raman Subba Row and David put on 202 for the third wicket and the match was won by six wickets. David's contribution was to make 239 not out. This won him a place in the England side for the Third Test against India at Old Trafford. He opened the batting with Len Hutton and made 34 before being out l.b.w. In the Fourth Test at the Oval he made 119, his first Test century.

At the end of the University year, David went back to play for Sussex—who finished the season with seven wins in a row. In the Autumn, he was invited to skipper the County side. The new season started with some low scores for the new captain and some poor results for Sussex. But by the end of May, the team started to play with confidence. A win against Leicester, in which David made 186 not out, was the beginning of a run in which they won seven out of ten matches and headed the County Championship table. Then they slumped and went for five matches without gaining a point. In the last match of the season, they beat Lancashire to finish runners-up in the Championship.

During his time at Cambridge, David had been considering what career to follow. 'I realised that God wants His servants in every walk of life, including cricket. In fact, there were so many opportunities of talking about the faith with individuals, and quite often to groups of young people, that I felt there was a strong case for finding a job which would allow me to stay in first-class cricket for some years. Cricketers and cricket followers, many of whom never went near churches, seemed able to talk about their questions and problems *because* I was involved in the life they understood.'

However, gradually David arrived at the conviction that God wanted him in the ordained Ministry of the Church of England. In 1953, he began two years' theological training at Ridley Hall, Cambridge. He imagined that he would play no more first-class cricket.

Throughout the Summer of 1954, the newspapers speculated on who would captain England for their Winter tour of Australia. One morning, David came down to the College common room to be shown banner headlines proclaiming the news that moves were afoot to persuade him to take the captaincy. The question of rivalling Hutton as prospective captain worried David, but in the event, it was Len Hutton who led the team that won the Ashes. However, David was called to take over the captaincy sooner than anyone anticipated. During the Summer, Hutton became ill after the First Test Match against Pakistan, and David was made captain for their next two matches. A fine win at Nottingham was followed by a draw at Manchester, where rain stopped play.

On 29 September 1955, David was ordained in St. Paul's Cathedral by the Bishop of London. For the next two years, he served as Assistant Curate at St. Mary's Church, Islington. The years he spent in Islington led him to feel deeply disturbed about the plight of working-class people. He came to realise how wide was the gap between the ordinary working people and the churches of all denominations. 'I was plunged into a different culture,' he says, 'and all my pre-suppositions had to be questioned.'

During his curacy he married his wife, Grace, who has always shared in and supported his ministry. There was a large number of West Indians and Nigerians living in the area, and David and Grace spent many hours visiting them. They also made a determined effort to make friends with their 'happy pagan' English neighbours and to demonstrate bit by bit that 'following Christ could be the most important and exciting adventure of their lives'.

It had been agreed that at the end of July, 1956, David should have a month free from his duties to play for Sussex. One afternoon early in the month, he went to Lord's to watch Cambridge play Oxford. Gubby Allen, who was Chairman of the England selectors, came across to him and said, 'Everyone's been telling me that I ought to press you to play, but I feel that if a man decides to pull out of cricket, that's his affair and you should leave him to it'. 'I'm playing a month's cricket for Sussex', David replied. 'Now you're talking', said Gubby, 'when are you starting?' When David told him that it was only the day before the team to play Australia was due to be selected, Gubby asked, 'Couldn't you play the match before that at Worcester? It would give us more chance to pick you!'

David was booked to speak at a school-leavers' service in Portsmouth, and Sussex were playing at Worcester the following day. David preached, and was up the next morning at 5 am to get to Worcester in time to make 59 for his county. On Saturday, he made 42 against Kent. When the news broke that he had been selected for the Third Test, the headlines announced that the young curate was being rushed from his parish with almost no practice to rescue England. It *was* like fiction become real. The *Daily Sketch* brought a coach-load of boys from the parish of Islington to Old Trafford. The game went well for England, Jim Laker breaking every world record for a bowler by taking nineteen wickets in the match. David himself hit 113 to help his team to a winning total of 459.

17

England went to the Oval for the last Test leading the series by two games to one. By Saturday morning, hot sun and a wet pitch made batting very hazardous. On a difficult wicket, David played one of his best innings, scoring 62. Rain interrupted play, and although the game was drawn, it resulted in England winning the Ashes.

The following year, 1957, the West Indies brought over a formidable team. David played against them for the MCC at Lord's and was brought into the England side for the last two Tests. In spite of lack of practice, he produced useful scores in each game.

During this time, the MCC team to tour South Africa was being selected. David was strongly opposed to the policy of apartheid. The cricket correspondent of one national 'daily' knew David's views and questioned him about his availability for the tour. David replied that he was not available 'because I have a lot of work to do in my job as a curate'. The next day, the paper carried a front page story under the headline, 'I WON'T PLAY IN AFRICA'. Soon after, he received a cutting from an African paper, *The Drum*, praising him for refusing to play in racially dominated cricket.

These events forced David to think hard about racial discrimination, and when the South Africans came to England in 1960, he again asked to be excused. He then consulted the Archbishop of Capetown and various other Christian leaders to enquire if it would help the cause of racial justice if he were to make public his decision not to play. His mind was finally made up when, in his daily reading from the Bible, one verse seemed to stand out, 'Cry aloud, spare not, lift up your voice like a trumpet; declare to my people their transgressions. . . . is not this the fast I choose: to loose the bonds of wickedness, to undo the thongs of the yoke, to let the oppressed go free, and to break every yoke?' David spoke out and, as a result, had to bear considerable criticism for 'bringing politics into cricket' *and* 'mixing politics with religion'.

Test cricket could have brought David offers of 'fashionable' parishes, but his two years in Islington had awakened him to the problems of the Church in working-class areas. He resolved to devote himself to tackle the task of inner-city mission, and to do this he knew it was essential to live where the people lived and to offer them long-term friendship and acceptance. The opportunity came when, in January 1958, he was appointed Warden of the Mayflower Centre, a Christian residential and community centre in East London's Canning Town.

The centre catered for all ages, but the largest number attending were between the ages of twelve and twenty-one. It was a hard task seeking to build bridges of under-standing. For instance, after appearing on the television programme *Sunday Break*, David walked into the Youth Club. 'Saw you on telly last night,' a girl said. 'Oh? Did you listen to what we were talking about?' 'Talking about cricket, weren't you?' 'Yes, and did you listen to the other part we were talking about?' 'Talking about God, weren't you?' 'Yes. What do you think about Jesus?' 'I don't know. I never saw Him, did I?'

David and Grace kept every Thursday evening free to visit non-church couples. Many children came to the centre, and this gave a point of contact with their parents. Gradu-ally, couples began to return these visits and came to the Sheppard's flat. 'We rarely talked narrowly about religious things, but towards the end of the evening, I made a point of having a half-hour discussion on some moral issue or a problem from daily life.' After eighteen months, couples began coming to 'Searching Groups' for more specific discussion of Christianity. Some came to a personal faith and began to attend worship regularly.

Because of his many duties, David did not have time to play much serious cricket. When he did, he was dubbed 'the Rev.' In 1960, he was playing in an occasional match for Sussex against Nottinghamshire. He edged a ball from 'Bomber' Wells rather luckily past slip. Wells called down the wicket, 'Said your prayers well last night, Rev?' 'Why', replied David, 'didn't you say *your* prayers last night, then, Bomber?' 'No. I trust to luck,' Wells shouted back.

David did not trust in luck. He believed that his Christian faith should influence his game just as it did every other aspect of life. 'If I am asked what difference my Christian faith has made to the way I have played cricket, I think first about the pressures of the game, especially in big cricket. To believe that I am in the place where God wants me to be, and that he is beside me in it has helped me greatly to be relaxed and properly alive. On one occasion when batting for Sussex, I found myself growing very angry with the other side. It was a difficult wicket to score on and the field-placing seemed to me to be ultra-defensive. I am afraid some heated words were exchanged between me and the bowler. Anger has never improved my batting and, instead of making a hundred as I should have done, I got out for 92. One member of our side was all ready to 'stir it up'. But as I sat and thought of my behaviour as a Christian, I knew that I couldn't leave it at that. When the other team came off the field, I went into their dressing-room and apologised to the bowler in front of them all. He shook my hand, and we have been good friends ever since.'

It was the policy of the Mayflower Council to give their staff a long leave after several years' service; David's was due in 1962 and the MCC was touring Australia that Winter. David had played only nine matches for Sussex in the previous four years, and not one in 1962, but when it became known that he might be available for selection, Walter Robins, then chairman of the Selection Committee, was heard to say, 'If it's true, it's the best news for English cricket that I've heard for a long time.'

To get into practice, David recommenced playing for Sussex. His form was closely observed by a dozen or so cricket correspondents. In his first match against Oxford University, he made 108 and 55. But the newspaper head-lines covering the next match against Warwickshire ran: SHEPPARD OUT FOR 0. The Gentlemen v. Players was the last chance he had to prove himself. Once again he rose to the occasion and, this time, made a century. He also caught Peter Parfitt at backward short leg off a hook. Peter went back to the dressing-room and threw down his bat in disgust. 'Bad luck, Peter, lad,' quipped Freddie Trueman, the Players' captain, 'you should know the Reverend has more chance than most of us when he puts his hands together.' David had earned his place in the team.

He began well with 81 in his first innings against South Australia. At Melbourne, in the Second Test, he made a disastrous start. In front of a crowd of 70,000, he was l.b.w. for 0, and then missed two catches. He was determined to do better, and in the second innings reached 113, being run out on what might have been the winning run of the match.

In the Third Test the batting of the whole team failed and Australia won by eight wickets. David dropped catches, in both the Third and Fourth Tests. He was not allowed to forget these missed catches! Brian Johnston, the BBC cricket commentator, in his book, *It's Been a Lot of Fun*, tells of a young English couple who had recently settled in Australia. Their first baby was born during the Test series and the mother suggested that David should be asked to christen it. 'Not likely,' said the father, 'in his present form he'd be bound to drop it.'

Brian Johnston also recalls, 'With the Rev. David Sheppard in the team we were kept on our religious toes and not only attended early service but went to hear him preach in the Cathedral. He did this in every city and people used to come in from miles away in the outback to hear him and he always had a full house.'

The series built up to a climax for the Fifth Test at Sydney. The Australian fast bowlers soon realised that there was no pace to be had from the wicket and tried to make scoring as difficult as possible. David, who was opening the English batting, was an easy target for the crowd. 'Look out, Reverend, your congregation will be leaving.' 'Why don't you hit him out into the green pastures?' When he allowed a ball to pass through to the wicket-keeper, a voice boomed, 'And it came to pass'. He was just beginning to time the ball well, when a good diving catch from the bowler sent him back to the pavilion for 19. In the second innings, David was at his best, reaching 68 on a very difficult slow wicket. England declared at 268 for 8 and left Australia 241 runs to win in 240 minutes. It was too hard a task and the game died away in a draw, and with it the chance for England to return with the Ashes.

After saying farewell to the team, David stayed on in Sydney for two months. On Easter Day, he preached in Long Bay Jail in the morning and the Cathedral at night. This was the beginning of a strenuous programme of meetings and services; he insisted that part of the time was spent in industrial areas similar to his own in London. As he saw some of the inner city districts and new housing estates of Sydney and Melbourne, he became convinced that Christian families must be prepared to stay in these depressed areas, or even move into them in order to establish strong neighbourhood churches. Cricket often proved a way to open up conversation. It was feared that when David went to the locomotive workshops at Everleigh, he would get a cold reception. The first man he encountered went through the motions of dropping a catch—everyone laughed. Later, two hundred men came during their lunch-break to hear David speak about Christ.

The match at Sydney was David's last in first-class cricket. After returning to England he found that his work at the Mayflower Family Centre left little time for sport. He could spare only three or four days a year for cricket, which did not provide sufficient practice for him to play well, and this he found frustrating. Furthermore, there was no suitable club conveniently near and so he decided to retire. Far from losing his love of cricket, David found that when he gave up playing, he recaptured the enthusiasm of earlier years as a 'dedicated follower' of the game. While the memories of his playing days were still fresh, he was persuaded to recount his cricketing experiences in a book entitled *Parson's Pitch*, published in 1964.

David stayed at the Centre for twelve years. 'It was a marvellous job. It changed me—it was almost as though I had a second conversion at Canning Town. I came to realise that God's interest is not just for the individual but is also for whole groups of people. God's concern is for justice and mercy, and in the Bible he is seen with a kind of built-in bias to the disadvantaged.'

David's own deep concern for social justice made him a fierce opponent of racialism. Even in the gentlemanly world of cricket, it led him into head-on conflict with the supporters of apartheid. In 1968 the MCC were to play in South Africa. Before the English team was selected, Basil D'Oliveira seemed an automatic choice as he had just played an innings of 158 against Australia. When the team was announced, however, his name had been omitted. To many people the reason appeared obvious—D'Oliveira was a Cape South African. David was on holiday in Belgium when he heard the news over the radio. He was very upset and hurried home to protest. As he was a member of the MCC Committee, he called a meeting, at which he was given a very 'rough ride'. He proposed a vote of no confidence which was seconded by a young, then little known player, Mike Brearley. Although the *vote* was lost, David felt that the *argument* had been won. Later, however, D'Oliveira was selected and this led to the cancellation of the tour.

In 1969, David had moved across the Thames to become the Bishop of Woolwich, as suffragan to the Bishop of Southwark. He had responsibility for the eastern half of the diocese from the Greenwich dockside to the commuter belt of east Surrey, one hundred and fifty parishes in all. David was worried that, as a Bishop, he might be 'taken out of the firing line', destined to meet only top people. He took the job determined to maintain contact with those outside the 'circle of power'. His family, now enlarged by the birth of Jenny in 1962, deliberately chose to live in working-class Peckham, 'in a rambling Victorian house in a side street off the Old Kent Road, so as not to be remote from ordinary people'.

In 1970, when South Africa was due to come to England, there was a considerable volume of protest. David was one of those who formed a 'Fair Cricket Campaign' which, although it was a moderate, non-disruptive group, nonetheless resulted in his receiving much bitter criticism and abuse. Even this was not without its moments of light relief. At a meeting of the MCC an elderly member stood up and made a vigorous attack on David, concluding, 'I don't know how the Bishop of Woolwich can wear his MCC tie'. A voice from the gallery shouted, 'Down his back!'

While he was at the Mayflower Centre, David's interest in the task of the Church in the inner areas of large cities had led him to begin collecting material for a book; his new appointment provided additional subject matter. The book was finally published in 1974 under the title *Built as a City—God and the Urban World Today*.

Because of his wide experience in urban areas and his understanding of the work of the Church in such circumstances, David was appointed Bishop of Liverpool in June 1975, one of the most important dioceses of the Church of England. The diocese is made up of two contrasting areas: Liverpool itself with its famous football teams *and* its problems of unemployment, vandalism and inner-city decline; and the surrounding towns of Lancashire, some with long histories, others only recently built. The Bishop has two hundred and twenty-two parishes and three hundred clergy under his pastoral care. His open, friendly manner, together with an evangelical faith and a lack of ecclesiastical pomp, have enabled him to reach groups often cut off from the normal work of the Church—not always with total approval, however. David recalls, 'An article about me in one of the Liverpool papers quoted a clergyman from one of the plushier parishes who said, "Unless you are poor, black and unemployed David Sheppard doesn't want to know you". This isn't true; I try to do a steady round of all the parishes and of all sorts of groups, but in a curious, back-handed way it was more of a compliment than it was intended to be!'

David has reached a wider audience through a weekly column in *Woman's Own*, which he wrote for seventeen years, and also through television. His most effective appearance was with his wife soon after their arrival in Liverpool in a programme called *The Bishop and the Dockers*. Grace spoke frankly and courageously about her two major illnesses, and in the ensuing discussion both husband and wife revealed a humanity which brought an unprecedented response of letters from viewers. 'I think what happened was that people who had always imagined that Christian leaders—indeed, Christians in general, were somehow above such stress, saw that we were not immune. A Christian does not cease to be a human being. The promise of Christ's salvation is not to protect us from all suffering and remove any possibility of failure, but that he forgives us and enters in to all those hurts beside us.'

David is passionately concerned for the poor and underprivileged. This is clear from his many public pronouncements and from his book, *Bias to the Poor*, published in 1983. In April 1984, he gave the Richard Dimbleby Lecture before an invited audience at the Royal Society of Arts in London. The Bishop asked everyone in what he called 'Comfortable Britain' to stand in the shoes of the people who live in the 'Other Britain'—city areas where poverty and unemployment are realities. He then went on to explain why attitudes must change, why politicians must alter their policies and why the Church must become involved. He concluded by making his own practical proposals for removing the relative poverty which 'imprisons the spirit' and divides the nation.

Although David has not played a proper game of cricket since 1972, he has coached the first eleven at a local Comprehensive School. He goes occasionally to watch a County game and manages about one day a year watching a Test Match. Nevertheless, he remains an 'enthusiastic follower at a distance'! Sometimes someone will say, 'You must miss cricket very much'. The reply David Sheppard gave soon after his retirement from first-class cricket is still applicable: 'Not really. Our life stretches us and absorbs us so much that there is not time to regret what else we might be doing. As with so many things in the Christian life, it has not been so much a case of "giving it up", as of "taking up" something else which is infinitely worthwhile'.

For further reading:

Parson's Pitch: David Sheppard, Hodder & Stoughton, 1964; Pbk 1968
Built as a City: David Sheppard, Hodder & Stoughton, 1974; Pbk 1975
Bias to the Poor: David Sheppard, Hodder & Stoughton, 1983.

2: Getting to Grips

Michael Brooks: Wrestling Parson

<u>Born 13 June 1935</u>

Mike Brooks had won his fight and was signing autographs. A small scruffy Yorkshire lad, having no autograph book, handed him a cigarette packet to sign. Mike tore it open and wrote 'To Jim, God Bless, from Michael A. Brooks'. The boy held out his grubby hand and said, 'Thanks Rev. and good luck wi yer Vicaring an all that.'

It is not often that one meets a minister of religions who is also a professional wrestler. It all began for Mike in the Lancashire village of Overton, with its view over the hills of the Lake District. In the summer, most of the villages held a Sports Day, which included wrestling in the 'Cumberland and Westmorland' style.* When he was not yet twelve, Mike won five shillings in savings stamps at the Overton Sports. Although he did not win another prize for over three years, that first victory fired his enthusiasm to go on to greater things. Every Wednesday he would travel a long distance to get some tuition and practice at the 'Caton Wrestling Academy'—a grandiose title for a few mats on the floor of a village hall! However, the training paid dividends and at the age of seventeen, he was placed third in the under-eighteen World Championship at Kendal.

Mike left school before he was fifteen and began work on a farm. In his spare time, he attended the Lancaster

---

*Each wrestler locks arms behind his opponent's back. A fall is gained when one wrestler touches the ground with any part of the body except the foot, or if he lets go his hold.

Lads's Club where he learned Free Style wrestling.* He soon mastered the new style and won the Northern Association of Boys' Clubs Championship when sixteen, as well as various other Northern competitions.

Mike became a professional wrestler by accident. In his eighteenth summer he and some of the lads from the Club followed a fair which included a wrestling booth. They were paid £3 for staying in the ring with the fair's regular wrestler. Unfortunately, the British Amateur Wrestling Association heard of their activities and banned them from all further amateur competitions on the grounds that they were now professionals.

Growing up near the mountains and sea had helped to persuade Mike of the existence of a God who was Creator and Architect of all beauty. He also accepted the fact of the life, death and resurrection of Jesus Christ, but it meant little to him personally and he had long given up regular attendance at church.

One Sunday evening, Mike went to Lancaster to train. As no one else turned up, he wandered back towards the bus station where he met a slight acquaintance who gave him a religious tract and pressed him to attend an after-Church youth rally. During the service, he began to feel uncomfortable; the words of the preacher seemed to be aimed directly at him. Some of the teenagers present spoke of what Jesus had done for them and how their lives changed when they were 'saved'. Mike was not too sure what 'being saved' meant, but he realised it was something worthwhile, which he had not experienced. So what must he do?

He relates what happened next in his book, *Wrestling with God:* 'I was told to surrender my life to Christ, to trust in Him as my Saviour. At the end of the service, those who wanted to accept Jesus Christ into their lives were invited

---

*Fought in rounds, using a variety of holds. A win is achieved by the first two of three falls, submissions, or a knock-out.

to go to the back of the hall where someone would come to counsel them. I stayed, I got converted, I was born again and Jesus became real to me.'

Next morning at work he started singing one of the choruses he had heard the night before. The farmer who employed him came out and asked, 'What's up with you, yer bin ter t'chapel or something'?' 'Yes, I got converted last night,' Mike replied.

The news that he had become a Christian soon spread and people noticed how he was now in control of a quick and sometimes violent temper. His whole life began to change, he felt a new sense of purpose and direction, and a real thrill in living. 'I was no longer at war within myself. Jesus made me a whole person.'

Mike joined the Sulyard Street Methodist Church in Lancaster. Three weeks after his conversion, he gave his testimony at a Church meeting and then began to go out with a Methodist lay preacher to help take part in leading Worship. As he studied to prepare for the pulpit and to take the exams that were needed for him to become a fully accredited Local Preacher, he was constantly challenged by new ideas. He came to believe that war was never justified in any circumstances. He registered as a Pacifist and instead of doing National Service in the Armed Forces he went to nurse at Lancaster Moor, a large psychiatric hospital. In his spare time, in addition to wrestling, he helped to run the youth club at his church. It was during this time that he bagan to feel a call to full-time ministry.

With National Service over, he worked for a year as a representative for a firm of agricultural merchants, but his mind kept turning to the ministry and he knew a decision had to be made. One night he prayed, 'Lord, show me this week what I must do. I'll be looking for a sign from you.' Nothing dramatic happened, except that on Thursday, while reading the *Methodist Recorder*, he came across an article on South Africa which concluded, 'If anyone is considering offering themselves as a candidate for the ministry, would they consider the need in South Africa?'

He applied, was interviewed, and accepted. It was felt that his wrestling ability would give him many useful contacts with the sports-loving people of South Africa. A month later, in June 1960, he disembarked at Cape Town.

The train journey to Windhoek, where Mike was to be based, took two and a half days. No sooner had he arrived than he was asked to conduct a service for the Superintendent Minister who had gone to take a funeral over five hundred miles away. When the Superintendent returned, Mike learned from him what his duties were to be. He was to travel across the centre of South West Africa for two weeks each month and to be in Windhoek for two weeks; there he was to be in charge of youth work. Although he was only a candidate for the ministry, he was granted a dispensation to administer the Sacraments of Baptism and the Lord's Supper in the absence of the Reverend Roy Fraser, the senior minister.

Life was so busy, so new and exciting that Mike had almost forgotten about wrestling—until the visit to Windhoek of 'Sky High Lee', the 7'3" Texan. The excitement of the crowd was infectious and during the interval Mike approached the promoter and told him that he would like to compete as a middleweight. Three weeks later, he was back in the same hall fighting Jan 'Ripper' Barnard, and just managed to win by gaining the only fall of the bout.

After the match, Mike was visited in the changing room by an official of the South West African Wrestling Board of Control, who told him that he had just beaten the South West African middleweight champion. A return bout for the title was arranged and Mike began regular training.

'When the night came for the championship contest, I was very nervous and I prayed that I might stay calm enough to do the best I was capable of. I never pray to win, just to be able to do my best and use all the abilities God has given me. The medical was over, I had been weighed in at 174 pounds, and now the officials were calling for the next contestants to come into the hall. The spectators in South West Africa and South Africa were very vocal but always fair, and as I entered the stadium they encouraged me with loud cheering, even though I was from England and my opponent was a local man bred and born and was an Afrikaaner. "Seconds out, round one," was the last thing I can remember hearing, and as for the fight, all I can now recall was that I won and was so excited about it that I didn't sleep that night even though I was tired out.'

Mike was now middleweight champion of South West Africa, a title he was to hold until his return to England in 1970. For nine years he was able to represent South West Africa in all their international competitions. These were mostly with other African countries, such as Angola, Zambia, Rhodesia, Mozambique and the Republic of South Africa, but also included matches with visiting teams from West Germany and France.

At first wrestling was, for Mike, a hobby and form of recreation, just as others might play tennis or golf. But as time went on, he began to realise the way in which it could extend his ministry. Wrestling was already giving him contact with many people right outside the church. People began to attend services out of curiosity, young lads came from the gymnasium where he trained to the Wesley Guild, a meeting he ran for young people, and he made many more new contacts at the Zoo Cafe where he ate out once a day. No one had come across a wrestling parson before!

Nic Visagie was one of those who trained with him at the gym. One Sunday evening Mike saw him in his congregation. 'At the close of the service as we were singing the last hymn, I asked anyone who felt they should surrender their life to the Lord Jesus and accept Him as Saviour, to come and kneel with me at the Communion rail. Nic was one of the first to come forward.' Nic was the welterweight boxing champion of South West Africa and also the lead guitarist in a Hotel band. He began to write new hymns to sing to 'pop' tunes, and also led some others from the band to experience a new life in Christ.

31

In February 1962, Mike went to Grahamstown, South Africa, to begin three years' theological training at Rhodes University. At the end of his second year, he wanted to visit his family in England. The only way to pay for the fare was by 'wrestling his passage'. It was an eventful, though not a restful holiday. On his return, the University student newspaper, the *Rhodeo*, wrote: 'Towards the end of last year Lancaster born Mike Brooks felt that he would like to see home again. For a man with a wrestling career that included Northern Counties Cup and Coronation Games Gold medal, this was easy. He got into contact with the European Wrestling Alliance in Britain who came to an agreement with him.

'Soon Mike was winging his way to England in a luxury jetline. In England he had thirty-five fights within the space of seven weeks. Of these fights he won eighteen, lost twelve and drew five, but even this was enough to help pay for his plane fare, a hired car, Christmas presents for all the family at home and some pocket money.

'In the course of his wrestling vacation, Mike wrestled against such people as Chic Purvey, the middleweight champion of Scotland, Tommy Mann, middleweight champion of Britain and Mike Donlevy, champion of the Republic of Ireland. He won two out of three of these important fights.

'Back at Rhodes Mike confessed that although his programme had been rather full, what with wrestling, sightseeing and preaching on Sunday, he still enjoyed every minute of it and strongly recommended a wrestling holiday to anyone wishing to go places cheaply.'

When he had finished the final year of his ministerial training at Rhodes, Mike did some more wrestling. It was a successful tour, during which he beat the Spanish middleweight champion in Beira, and won all but one of his contests in the Republic of South Africa. In the Cape Town City Hall he lost to Blondie Pienaar, the welterweight champion of South Africa. Although on one occasion he managed to hold him to a draw, Pienaar was the only South African wrestler around his weight that Mike was unable to beat. This was not surprising in the circumstances—a theological student, spare-time wrestler, up against a former Olympic silver medallist and winner of a gold medal in the Common-wealth Games.

Following this wrestling tour, Mike spent the remainder of the summer vacation around Cape Town before returning to Walvis Bay, a small town on the Skeleton coast. There he began work as a probationer minister. He had pastoral care of the whole of the northern part of South West Africa, an enormous section stretching approximately four hundred miles in each direction. About half of each month was spent in and around Walvis Bay where he had a flat, and during the other half he travelled the area further north.

There was much to be done. The work at Walvis Bay prospered, at Tsumeb a school was acquired and converted into a dual purpose church hall, regular services were commenced at the township of Kuisebmund. There was also the Free Church Chaplaincy at the military base at Walvis Bay and always there were long journeys on rough and lonely roads through the bush. These were accomplished in a Volkswagen—until the day its engine blew up. As he was overdrawn at the bank and still paying instalments on the car itself, Mike was unable to afford the almost-new engine he was offered. The only means of paying was another wrestling tour.

With three weeks of holiday due, Mike put himself in the hands of promoter 'Bull' Hefer, who sent him an air ticket for Johannesburg. After a round trip by road and air covering over 1000 miles, Mike began his tour by winning the first match at Germiston. He then travelled up to Belfast in Northern Transvaal where he fought Willie van der Walt, the middleweight champion of the Transvaal and a top-class wrestler. After seven gruelling rounds, Mike was only just able to stand for the referee to raise his hand as the victor. Afterwards he lay in the changing room for over an hour before he recovered. Back to Johannesburg's Wembley Stadium where he met Johnny 'Golden Boy'

Botha, a very rough, showy wrestler. It was another very hard contest and it was not until the last minute of round eight that Mike gained the only fall to win the match.

The following day, Sunday, Mike attended worship at the Methodist Central Hall and then, with two other wrestlers, set off for Cape Town, over a thousand miles away. During the night the car developed trouble with the generator and eventually the engine stopped. For a couple of hours the three men pushed it uphill and coasted it downhill. Eventually one of them walked on ahead to get help. At six o'clock in the morning they were towed into a garage and, after repairs, set off again, arriving about midday having had no proper sleep. Not surprisingly, all three lost their bouts that evening.

The next matches were in Natal. On the long journey there the exhaust pipe fell off the car and had to be secured with wire taken from a roadside fence. The temperature was below zero and they drove with the windows tight shut. When they arrived in the early hours, the three wrestlers staggered out of the car like drunken men—unbeknown to them, the exhaust fumes had been seeping through the floor. The next day they awoke feeling sick and dizzy. In the evening Mike wrestled with Gert Niewoudt, the middleweight champion of Natal. It was a close contest which Mike felt he was lucky to win, particularly after his opponent put him in a sleeper hold. The pressure on his neck brought back the carbon monoxide 'hangover', and he looked so ill that a lady in the audience shouted out, 'Do yer want an aspirin, luv?'

A tag match* win at Pietermaritzburg was followed by a hard fought victory over the middleweight champion of the Orange Free State. Then came the long journey back to Johannesburg, a journey not without incident. Mike,

---

*A match with two teams of two, where one team member is in the ring and the other one outside. They change places when they touch or 'tag' each other.

wearing his clerical collar, was driving, while a French wrestler and a big Portuguese were asleep in the back; in the other front seat sat Frikkie Alberts, a heavyweight champion who, at that time, wore a black mask and wrestled under the name 'Vrystaat'. They pulled in at a filling station for petrol and while they were there, a bus full of Africans drew in. One of them saw the sinister figure in a black mask sitting by a man in a clerical collar, screamed wildly and jumped back on the bus. Others on the bus looking out saw what they thought was a car full of gangsters, leapt off the bus and ran in terror down the road. The petrol pump attendant also took one look and fled, screaming, into the bush.

After another week of wrestling Mike came to the Pretoria City Hall for his last match of the tour. It was with the middleweight champion of the Republic of South Africa, Maans Groenwalt. It was one of those fights that Mike remembers with great pleasure. Maans was a fine wrestler and at the end of eight five-minute rounds there was no score. The officials went into the ring and asked the wrestlers if they would continue another round and try for a decision. Mike won with a pin fall. The hall seemed to explode with a mighty roar as he helped Maans to his feet and was announced the winner in extra time. People leapt into the ring to shake hands and hug the two contestants and eventually they were both carried shoulder high to their dressing rooms.

The following day Mike arrived back in Windhoek tired, but happy with the knowledge that he had earned enough to buy a new engine for his car. A few days after his return he was off again on his travels—preaching and visiting, over the large area under his pastoral care.

A year later, having driven thousands of miles over rough gravel roads, the car was again in need of expensive repairs. 'Bull' Hefer arranged another wrestling tour, which once more concluded with a match against Maans Groenwalt. In the third round Mike went down backwards from a leg snatch and hit his head on the corner of the ring. He banged it again when he lost a fall in the fourth round. The next thing he remembered was sitting in the changing room. A board of Control official came in, shook his hand and congratulated him. Mike looked very surprised and said, 'But I haven't been on yet.' 'Yes, you have, it was a fantastic fight,' the official replied. 'How did I get on then?' Mike asked. 'It was a draw, you got a wonderful fall, so fast I can't explain it.' No doubt due to the effects of concussion, those last four rounds and the equalising fall have remained a complete void in Mike's memory. The following day he was back in South West Africa, after another strenuous but profitable three weeks' 'holiday'.

In spite of the generosity of his Churches, the mission was always short of funds. Mike arranged for a touring team of wrestlers to come to his area and the church to handle the promotions, thereby taking a percentage of the profits. Many of the top wrestlers from South Africa took part. Mike was always assured of plenty of support. The local paper reporting on one bout said, 'At one stage, when the Free State wrestler Johann Slabbert had been hurled right out of the ring into the audience, he tried to stagger weakly to his feet only to be felled again by a single blow with a shoe from a frail woman in the audience, and could she pack a punch!' She would have found it hard to understand that Mike and Johann were, in fact, good friends out of the ring.

Before his ordination Mike attended a further three months' course of ministerial training in Johannesburg; this also gave him the opportunity for some more wrestling. While on the course he was booked to preach at a Baptist Church in Johannesburg. As he stepped into the pulpit, he was surprised and thrilled to see one side of the church almost filled with wrestlers and their families. The next day, the newspapers carried the headline, 'Top South African wrestlers go to church'. The following night Mike was wrestling in Pretoria and was changing in the same dressing room as Martiens Jacobs, the 'Kalahari Wildman'. He told Mike that he and his wife had been deeply moved during

Sunday's service and had both admitted their personal needs and committed their lives to Christ. There in the changing room they knelt to pray.

As a result of his conversion, the 'Kalahari Wildman' became involved in a children's mission in the Methodist Church at Jepe, a run-down area of Johannesburg. The 'double three-o club' averaged a regular three hundred children, with some nine hundred on the final day when the 'Wildman' presented prizes. Six and a half feet tall and weighing eighteen and a half stones, he towered above parents and children. Each child was given a New Testament, the 'Wildman' having paid for these and the cakes and coke served that afternoon.

Mike was ordained as a Methodist Minister in October, 1966 in the Metropolitan Methodist Church, Capetown. He then returned to South West Africa where he continued his preaching and pastoral work, fitting in wrestling contests whenever there was the time and opportunity. He remained undefeated Middleweight champion of South West Africa. His most memorable fights were against Maans Groenwald, the current South African champion; they were always close fought bouts, some he lost, some were drawn and some he won.

In 1970 Mike returned to England, where he had eight months to wait before commencing work in the British Methodist Church. He spent this period wrestling as a full-time professional and fought a number of wrestlers made famous by their television appearances. He had two good wins over the Southern Area champion, Peter Rann, a couple of wins against 'TV' Jackie Pallo and lost in two encounters with Mick McManus. One of these took place before 6,000 spectators in Paisley Ice Rink on January 19, 1970. Among Mike's supporters were two coach loads of residents from a Glasgow Corporation home for the elderly, where he had preached on the previous Sunday. They cheered mightily when Mike scored a pin fall against McManus and booed loudly when, in round five, McManus scored the winning fall by somewhat dubious tactics. At one point in the contest, a lady in the front row was brandishing her shoe at McManus and threatening what she would do to him if he dared to come out of the ring. McManus ducked under the ropes and glaring down at her yelled, 'I'll bet you go to his church as well'.

Scotland is one of the world's greatest wrestling countries and the Highland Games have produced some outstanding wrestlers. One of Mike's best achievements was to come second in the middleweight championships of 1975, only being beaten by Alan Richardson who, at that time, had won the Games four times in succession. Because Mike was often matched as the 'goodie' versus the 'baddie', he usually had the crowd on his side. On one occasion, this proved embarrassing when he was nearly involved in a riot at the Kelvin Arena, Glasgow. Mike's contest was last on the bill, and during the earlier bouts he had been sitting in the audience chatting with some of the spectators. He was matched against Eric Cutler, one of the 'Black Diamonds', and known as a tough, rough fighter. In the third round, Cutler made what was probably an unintentional foul. Mike took his time in getting up in order to get his wind back, and before he was on his feet the crowd was in the ring protesting vociferously. The police were called to clear the ring and the match was resumed. A minute later, Mike was floored by another foul, and as he lay on the canvas he heard the referee urgently whisper, 'Get up quick, punch him or kick him'. Mike was so surprised and bemused that he did as he was told and swung a couple of punches at his opponent and delivered a mule kick. The referee declared it no contest and stopped the match. 'Thanks for doing that', he whispered, 'we'd never get out of here tonight if you hadn't'. The next moment, despite the police, the spectators were in the ring. Mike was hoisted shoulder high and carried in triumph round the hall and right up to the gallery!

In August 1970, Mike married his wife, Pauline, and in September he was appointed by the British Methodist Church to the Newcastle-upon-Tyne West circuit. There he spent seven 'tremendously happy years' in a predominantly working class area. Because of his involvement in the world of wrestling, Mike was given a warm welcome in Working Men's Clubs, School Assemblies, Youth Clubs and other non-church organisations. He found that often the rougher element, the so-called 'drop-outs', were the most eager to talk to him. 'It's amazing how quickly people will come and talk about their problems and sometimes about their desire for a relationship with the Church and with Christ. They may have wished many times previously to have talked to a minister, but just hadn't the nerve to approach one. Seeing me wrestle seems to make them feel I'm more on their level; the wrestling acts as a bridge between them and the Church.'

Often a conversation would be started when someone came to ask for an autograph. A lad from Gateshead asked Mike to sign his book after he had wrestled Jackie Pallo in Newcastle City Hall. A few minutes later he came back to ask why Mike had put, 'God Bless'. After Mike had explained, the youngster wandered away, then came back again, handed Mike five pence and said, 'Put that into your church collection for me, please'. A moment after he returned yet again and asked, 'How do you get to your church?' Two weeks later he was in the congregation.

The Newcastle *Journal* reported the Jackie Pallo fight under the headline, 'Here endeth the lesson': 'Hundreds of fans, most of them supporting the wrestling parson, packed into Newcastle's City Hall for what was billed as the star bout of the evening. The fight was packed with action right from the first round, although Pallo seemed to think that he was going to have a very easy time of it. Taking Mr. Brooks in a head lock, Pallo warned him "Start praying now Vicar". Then in the second round, Pallo stopped wrestling to sign his autograph for a lady sitting at the ringside. He showed that his early confidence was not misplaced by pinning Mr. Brooks to the canvas for a count of three to gain the first fall in the third round. But then, in round five. Pallo received a public warning for fouling and Mr.

Brooks seized the opportunity to pin him to the canvas for the equaliser.

'Then in the sixth, came the incident which led to Pallo being disqualified and the crowd roared their approval as the referee raised Mr. Brooks' hand in victory. Charitable to the last, Mr. Brooks took the microphone and told the crowd that he was sure that Jackie Pallo would not have fouled him on purpose and it must have been an accident.

'But, he added, even if the contest had not been stopped, he was sure that he would have beaten Pallo. He was willing to fight him again any time, anywhere. Pallo replied that if Mr. Brooks preached as well as he wrestled then his congregation would be well looked after. He said he would be willing to meet him again as long as the fight did not take place in Newcastle where the crowd was biased.

'To mark his victory, Mr. Brooks was presented with a cheque for £250 by the Newcastle building firm of William Leech to donate to a charity of his choice.'

Before leaving Newcastle, Mike was asked to write a book about his wrestling experiences. It was published in 1976 entitled, *Wrestling for God*. In September 1977, Mike moved to the Carlisle Methodist circuit, where he took charge of the Carlisle Central Hall and three smaller churches. He found that wrestling had been discontinued in Carlisle, but soon after his arrival a promoter 'phoned to ask if he could get it started again. In consequence, the Market Hall, conveniently opposite his largest church, was soon packed out for monthly Friday night wrestling contests. Mike, when not wrestling, acted as time-keeper or referee.

Mike's first fight in Carlisle came about in unusual circumstances. During a tag match at which Mike was scoring, the referee was knocked over by the wrestlers, and while he was on the canvas, Tally-Ho Kaye, a tough, horse-riding wrestler from Lancashire put his opponent in a fall position and shouted to the referee to start counting. The referee counted the fall, but then questioned round the ring as to whether it was a fair move. Mike, wearing, as usual, his clerical collar, went into the ring to give the final verdict, stating that, in his opinion, it was a foul. Tally-Ho Kaye was furious and threw a punch at Mike who, to Kaye's surprise, caught him and threw him back across the ring. When he had recovered, Kaye challenged Mike to a fight, boasting that he could beat him with one hand tied behind his back. Mike accepted the challenge.

In preparation for the match, Mike went into serious training, which included a trip to Ireland. Taking Services on the Saturday and Sunday and fitting in a number of schools' visits during the week, Mike fought five contests during the next five days, achieving three draws and two wins—one over the Irish middleweight champion.

Two days before the scheduled contest with Tally-Ho Kaye, Mike received a 'phone call from William Leech, the Newcastle builder, who asked him how he fancied his chances. 'Pretty good', Mike replied. 'Alright', said the builder, 'if you win I'll give you £250 for any charity you wish to name'. On the night of December 8, 1978, the Market Hall was filled to capacity with over two thousand people, and the event was covered by local radio and Border Television. Full of confidence, Kaye won the first fall, but Mike evened the score and then, in the fourth round, clinched the fight with a crotch-hold fall. Mr. Leech donated the promised £250 and a further £23 was given by the crowd. The total cheque for £273 was handed to the Christian Aid representative for Cumbria at a civic carol service held at the Central Hall and attended by the Mayor and Mayoress of Carlisle.

The following year, several local firms sponsored Mike in a return match with Tally-Ho Kaye. Once again the battling parson won and, as a result, at the annual carol service, £520 was presented to Mike for work among young people. Mike continued wrestling into 1981 and one of his main events was when he partnered 6ft 1in, 25 stone 'Big Daddy' in a Tag Match against 'Banger' Walsh and 6ft 11in, 35 stone 'Giant Haystacks'.

Later that year, Mike was struck down with rheumatoid

arthritis. The illness came on very suddenly and affected every part of his body, even his jaw. One week he was training hard, three weeks later he was unable even to drive his car. Although his condition has improved considerably, Mike has had to retire from the ring. For a while he attempted to referee, but found that he could not move quickly enough to do the job properly. However, he is still involved with the world of wrestling, from time to time acting as a popular Master of Cermonies.

Recently, Carlisle's wrestling minister took on another challenge—to raise £26,000 for essential maintenance work on the Methodist Central Hall in Fisher Street where he was minister*. One of his most successful fund-raising ventures has been a 'Wrestling Charity Spectacular', arranged in conjunction with Dale Martin Promotions. Mike was M.C. and top of the bill was a bout between Ireland's World Champion 'Fit' Finlay and British Light-Heavyweight, Marty Jones.

The people who hear Mike preach welcome his involvement in wrestling. When actively wrestling, the women were among his most enthusiastic supporters, often hiring coaches to go to support him. One of his fans, a dear old lady, so frail that Mike was almost afraid to shake her hand, when leaving church one day, put her clenched fists up to her face and said, 'Next time you are in the ring with that McManus, give him one of these'!

Sometimes he has been able to say a few words from the ring. At Christmas time, for instance, he has given greetings to the spectators from the wrestlers and then reminded the crowd whose birthday it is and asked them to make room in their hearts and in their celebrations for Jesus Christ.

Sometimes there has been the opportunity to help a family rejoin the Church. One night after a match in Hull, a family who had given up worshipping sixteen years previously came to see him. They wanted to start again,

*Mike is now a minister in West Yorkshire.

but did not know what to do about it. A similar thing happened in Barrow-in-Furness. In each case, it seemed that it was easier for the people involved to talk to a minister they had just seen in the wrestling ring.

'Being a minister and being involved in wrestling are closely tied together in my experience', says Michael Brooks. 'I believe that God has used me to serve Him in the ring as well as the pulpit. The world of wrestling keeps me in touch with people outside the church, and it is a means of witness to people who would never come to church to hear the Christian gospel. When I was converted and gave my life to the Lord, it included my wrestling, and He has been able to use both, incredible as it may seem. I love the sport of wrestling, but I love my Lord far more and He must always come first.'

For further reading:

Wrestling for God: Mike Brooks, Christian Journals Ltd., 1976

3: Supreme Champion

Gary Player: International Golfer

Born 1 November 1935

Twenty year old Gary Player set himself six major goals: to have the lowest stroke average for a year on the United States professional golf tour, to be the top money winner on the US circuit for a year, and to win the four major world championships—the British Open, the American Masters, the United States PGA.* Championship and the United States Open Championship. When, later, he achieved all six goals, he knew that it was in no small measure due to the influence of his father and mother.

It was his father who taught him the importance of thinking positively and instilled in him the idea that strength of character comes from meeting and conquering adversity. Harry Player worked long, arduous hours deep underground in the gold mines near Johannesburg, South Africa. On the low wages he earned, it was always a struggle to provide adequately for his wife, daughter and two sons. Although Gary's mother died of cancer when he was only eight, she, too, had a profound influence on the development of his character. From her he learned the value of courtesy and thoughtfulness for others, and what it means to have faith in God and to find in that faith a blueprint for life. Each night his mother knelt by his bed as he said his prayers; from her he learned that there is a God who listens and who loves and cares for everyone.

Life was not easy, but Gary had the love and support of

*Professional Golfers Association.

his sister, Wilma and brother, Ian, and later, when his father married again, a stepmother. Ian did much to help him to develop not only physical fitness but also courage and determination. One day when they were on a five-mile run, Gary, unable to go any further, sank to the ground and gasped, 'Ian, I just can't make it. I can't go on'. Ian pulled him to his feet and retorted, 'You can do anything you want to. Remember that. There's no room for "can't" in this life'. It was a lesson he never forgot.

It was Ian also who, from a stick, whittled Gary's first golf club and taught him how to swing it. Later, his father took him out on to the local course and, to the surprise of them both, he managed to complete three consecutive holes in par*. At school Gary was a good all-round athlete, but golf was the sport he enjoyed most of all. His keenness was greatly increased when he met pretty Vivienne Verwey, whose father was the golf professional at Virginia Park Golf Course where Gary played. The second time he saw her he said to his stepbrother, 'Christopher, I'm going to marry that girl some day'. She was thirteen and he was fourteen. Before long they were 'going steady' and this gave Gary all the additional inspiration he needed to practise golf eight to ten hours every day. Already he had begun to dream of becoming a professional.

Gary had grown up with a firm belief in God. When he was fifteen he met Marcus Levy, an encounter that, although brief, had a profound influence on his life. In the book, *Gary Player World Golfer*, he recalls, 'Mr. Levy did two things that edged me towards a life-changing decision: he told me that with faith in God a person's life can be richer and have more meaning, that with faith incredible things can and will happen; then he gave me a little book which I read eagerly. I'm not certain now of the title, but I think it was *Faith in Christ*. At any rate, it was then that

---

*The number of strokes a scratch player (i.e. one with *no* handicap advantage) should require for a hole.

I had a conversion experience and accepted Christ into my life. . . . I came to see that God so loved me that He had sent His Son, Jesus Christ, to pay the penalty of my sins and give me a new life. When I realised this, everything changed and my first desire now was to serve God.'

It was also during his fifteenth year that a foolish prank brought all immediate participation in sport to an abrupt end. One afternoon, coming home from school, Gary and his friends were passing a deep compost pit. They decided it would be fun to run and jump into the cushion of decomposed grass and leaves which filled the hole. Gary took a long run and dived *head first* into the pit. His momentum carried him right through the layers of compost and he hit the bottom with such force that he was knocked unconscious and broke his neck. He was fortunate to survive at all, and recovery took a long time. There followed weeks of frustrating inactivity, and Gary chafed with impatience to be back on the golf course.

It was not until he was well past his sixteenth birthday that he was able to start playing again. For the next two years he spent every day playing and practising under the expert guidance of Mr. Verwey. He recollects: 'These were long years of painful struggle, of muscle-stretching work, of intense concentration. But I was determined to become good enough to play professional golf—and not just to play, but to win.' In 1953, at eighteen years of age, he turned professional. Moving in with the Verweys, he became assistant pro at Virginia Park. In addition to giving lessons to others, he practised at least eight hours every day. At times he wondered if his lack of height would be a serious handicap. One day he said to his father, 'Dad, I'm too small. I don't think I'll ever become a champion'. Gary never forgot his father's reply: 'Nonsense, it all depends on the guts you have. It's what's inside of you that matters, not what's on the outside'.

Gary had looked forward eagerly to the time when he might qualify to play in the major professional golf tournaments in South Africa. When the opportunity came there was only one problem—money. However, his father floated a bank loan for him and, in those early days, Gary tried to economise by using old golf balls. His clothes were so shabby that when he was invited to play an exhibition match with Peter Thompson and Bobby Locke, he borrowed a pair of trousers from Vivienne's brother—unfortunately, they were a couple of sizes too large and considerable ingenuity was required to keep them up!

In spite of the doubts of some members of his home club, Gary finished his first tour in the top twelve. His greatest thrill was to finish second in a tournament won by Bobby Locke—four times winner of the British Open and many other major tournaments. With the prize money he was just able to purchase his first car, although he left himself without enough money to buy the petrol to run it!

During 1953 and 1954, Gary's game inproved steadily, but the turning point came in 1955 when he won his first tournament on the South African circuit. He had by this time been appointed assistant pro at Killarney Golf Club, also in Johannesburg. The members generously took a collection to help finance his first foreign tour, and with a mixture of excitement and apprehension, Gary flew to Cairo for the Egyptian Match Play Championship. There were four other South African golfers taking part as well as some of the finest Egyptian players, and although the competition was fierce, Gary captured the title. The prize money for the winner enabled him to extend the tour by another two months and he came to England and the British golf circuit. After five months away and with barely enough money for his flight home, Gary returned to Johannesburg. 1955 had been a year to remember, the year in which he took his first steps to becoming a world golfer.

Early in 1956, Gary was back in England playing in the Dunlop Masters tournament at Sunningdale Golf Club in Surrey. It was another landmark in his career. The game became a duel between Gary and Arthur Lees, the Sunningdale professional, who had never been beaten on his home course. It was a five-round tournament and Gary won it with a total score of 338 for the 90–hole course, setting a world record for five rounds. Back home there was a further triumph when Gary had the satisfaction of winning his first South African Open Championship. As a result of these two successes, he received an invitation to go to Australia to play in the Ampol tournament.

By this time, Vivienne and Gary had been going out together steadily for six years. They wanted desperately to get married but could not afford to set up a home. Just before leaving for Melbourne, Gary reached a decision. 'Look,' he said, 'if I win, we'll get married right away. There are a lot of good American, British and Australian players entered in the tournament. I don't know whether I stand much chance, but I'm really going to try.' It was a closely contested tournament, but Gary finished the final round with a seven-stroke lead. He rushed from the course to send Vivienne a cable: 'Buy the wedding dress. We'll be married immediately.' On the morning of January 19, 1957, Gary played nine holes of golf; that same day, in the afternoon, at the Central Hall Methodist Church in Johannesubrg, he was married to Vivienne Verwey. It had been an eventful twelve months, made even more memorable by the fact that in 1956 Gary was first voted South African Sportsman of the Year—an honour he has received five times since. It was also the year when he first dreamed of becoming the best golfer in the world.

In 1957 came another breakthrough. Gary received an invitation to play in the United States, in the prestigious American Masters Tournament. Later he won the Australian PGA and, in 1958, in addition to several other important tournaments, the Australian Open. The following year, still lacking in professional experience and only twenty-three, he came to England determined to win the 1959 British Open played at Muirfield in Scotland. On the last day of play he was eight strokes behind the leaders and seemed to be out of the reckoning, but he finished well with a total score of 284 for the 72 holes. However, he had a long time to wait before knowing the final result as the leaders were playing two hours behind him. He suffered an agony of suspense until the last player holed out. He had won—by just two strokes. What was more, he had won the first of the four major championships comprising golf's Grand Slam. He recalls, 'This was one of the great moments of my life—a never-to-be-forgotten thrill . . . But with the first leg of the big four behind, my thoughts turned to the remaining three. At that point, it wasn't a question of whether or not it would happen, but when.'

His next major target was the American Masters Championship. 1960 was his third year of competition in this tournament and produced his best result yet—he tied for sixth place. Playing in his own country during the remainder of the season Gary did better, winning six major tournaments including the South African Open and the South African PGA. The following spring, he arrived at the Augusta National Golf Club in Georgia for his fourth attempt at the American Masters. His main rival was Arnold Palmer, the defending champion and the undisputed favourite for 1961. On a wet opening day of competition, Palmer came in with a 68 and Gary was only one stroke behind. On the second day the result was reversed, Gary playing five birdies, twelve pars and one bogey*. On the third round he made a good start with birdies on holes 1, 2, 6 and 8. Then he ran into trouble on the 420–yard 9th hole when a poor tee shot landed in the woods. In spite of bogies on holes 11, 12 and 13, he still finished with a score of 69 while Palmer took 73. Thus Gary started the fourth day with a four-stroke lead; however, a heavy rainstorm washed out play halfway through the round. The players waited in frustration for the game to resume on the following day. Gary played a disappointing round, finishing with a two-over-par 74 and a total of 280 for the tournament. At this stage Palmer, playing behind Gary, had a one

*Birdie: hole done in one *under* par, bogey: hole done in one *over* par.

stroke lead and, amid growing excitement, he held it until his final hole. Vivienne and Gary could hardly bear to watch that vital hole on television. A poor approach shot put Palmer in a bunker and it took him two more to get within fifteen feet of the hole. He was putting for a tie and a play-off seemed inevitable. Palmer missed the putt by inches and finished the tournament with a 281. The American Masters belonged to Gary by one stroke—and he was halfway towards the coveted four 'Majors'.

Winning consistently, week after week, is virtually impossible in golf, and Gary now struck a bad patch. He went fifteen months without a tournament win and even failed to qualify for the last two rounds of the 1962 British Open at Troon. On arrival at Aronimink Golf Club near Philadelphia for the forty-fourth American PGA tournament, he confided to a friend his intense feelings of frustration and a desire to give it all up and return permanently to South Africa. However, he realised his mental attitude was wrong and he decided to make one last attempt. 'After all', he reasoned, 'I'm only twenty-four, it's up to me to prove my career is not over.' Confidence flooded back and he began to recover his lost form. By the third round he was in the lead by two strokes. In the final round he held his lead until Bob Goalby, his playing partner, narrowed his lead to only one stroke. When Gary missed a thirty-foot putt, a tie seemed certain, but Goalby narrowly missed his putt and Gary holed his to finish one stroke up on his partner and three ahead of Jack Nicklaus. His outlook on the future was transformed for, as he says: 'Confidence had been restored and I was a new person, and instead of thinking about retiring, my thoughts zeroed in on the United States Open. Now, only this tournament blocked my goal of capturing all four of the big ones. The Grand Slam was within reaching distance'.

But when the 1963 United States Open was played in Massachusetts, Gary could only manage eighth place. The following year, in Washington, DC, he did not even finish in the first ten. During the two years that had elapsed since his PGA victory, Gary had won six tournaments and had been placed in the top ten 26 times. He had now achieved five of the six goals he had set for himself nine years previously. Only one goal remained; one all-important tournament still eluded him, and with it the Grand Slam.

In June 1965, the United States Open was played at Bellerive Country Club in St Louis. Jack Nicklaus and Arnold Palmer, both powerful hitters, were the favourites to win on this extra long, 7,191–yard course. On the way to the first tee on the opening day, Gary stopped for a few moments in front of the giant leaderboard. On it were the names of all previous US Open winners. At the top of the list was the 1964 champion, Ken Venturi. In imagination Gary saw something no one else could see. Above Venturi's name, he visualised the headline emblazoned in gold: *1965—Gary Player*. Briefly he prayed, 'Dear God, give me strength and courage to try my best and fight it out as hard as I can and to accept things in adversity'.

After the first two days of play, the 150–man field had been narrowed down to 50. Arnold Palmer and Ken Venturi, the defending champion, were eliminated, Jack Nicklaus was out of contention with 150 and Gary was on 140, one stroke ahead of Kel Nagle and Mason Rudolph. On Saturday the weather was warm and bright, the course in perfect condition, and Gary finished the day holding a two-stroke lead over Nagle. On the final day the play was as intense as the heat. After fifteen holes Gary's lead lengthened to three strokes, but at the 16th his tee shot went straight into a bunker, and before completing the hole he had taken two over par. Nagle birdied 17 and they were even. The 18th hole at Bellerive is a tough par–4. Gary had to make par to stay even, but a birdie would give him both the tournament *and* the four 'Majors'. He recalls those critical moments: 'My drive landed in excellent position on the right side of the fairway, and a 5–iron second shot came to rest on the green just fifteen feet from the hole. Then came that big moment of truth. After studying the greens,

I sighted the putt carefully, and then . . . it moved right along a line directly toward the cup but faltered to a stop just a fraction short. . . . At that moment I missed winning the United States Open Championship by one and one-half inches'. Gary tapped the ball in to tie with Nagle at 282 strokes.

This meant that there had to be an 18–hole play-off on the Monday. After four holes Gary was leading by one stroke. At the 5th hole Nagle's drive curved and hit a woman spectator on the head. Bleeding profusely she fell unconscious. Gary tried to reassure Nagle but he was unnerved and his next shot ricocheted off another woman's ankle. It was all over for Nagle and at the conclusion of the remaining thirteen holes, Gary was the clear winner by three strokes. America's biggest golf championship *and* the four 'Majors' were his. At that time, Gene Sarazen and Ben Hogan were the only other players to have won golf's four major championships, and now Gary had joined them. It was one of the greatest moments in his life. Three years before, Gary had made a promise that if he ever won the United States Open, he would donate his $25,000 winnings to charity. He now honoured that promise by donating $20,000 to the USGA to help promote junior golf and $5,000 to cancer research in memory of his mother.

Although his free time was very limited, Gary took the opportunity, whenever he could, of speaking to young people and church groups. He also enjoyed meeting with and speaking to groups within the Fellowship of Christian Athletes, an active organisation of sports people in the United States. One of his speaking engagements was to address thirteen thousand ministers and representatives of the 1967 Southern Baptist Convention in Miami, Florida. It was here that he received one of the greatest honours of his career as a golfer: the 'Christian Athlete of the Year' award. In his address he spoke of God as 'a partner in my life. And, as with any partnership, I'm sure he disapproves of some of the things I do and think. Still, the strength and guidance and motivation for everything I do comes from Him'.

Gary has been much influenced in his religious thinking my two men. First, there is Dr. Norman Vincent Peale, a minister who, through his writing and preaching stresses the need to set goals and visualise positive results. Then, there is the evangelist, Dr. Billy Graham, who has helped Gary to a better understanding of the practicalities of prayer. To Gary the most important thing about prayer is that 'God does hear and care about what we feel and say. I'm very conscious of his presence in my life. And this is an absolutely tremendous thing when I think of the wonder and vastness of our marvelous and complex universe. It's almost unbelievable to think that the Creator of all this is concerned about me, Gary Player, and my needs'.

The seasons 1966 and 1967 were something of an anticlimax; the only important championship Gary won was the Piccadilly World March Play Championship in 1966. But in July 1968 he again won the British Open—nine years after his first win. He went on to win six more tournaments in 1968, including the World Series of Golf in Akron, Ohio and, for the third time, the Piccadilly World Match Play Championship at Wentworth, England.

One of the severest tests to Gary's faith and character took place during the 1969 and 1970 seasons when, on several occasions during the US golf tour, he was picketed and subjected to vicious abuse. Although the demonstrations were really directed against the apartheid policies of the government of South Africa and not against Gary personally, nonetheless 'the protest as it finally emerged was directed at me as a person without taking into consideration that I am not a racist and that I work constantly for understanding and improved relations between all races everywhere, and especially in my home country'.

Nevertheless, 1969 proved a successful year for him. He played in sixteen United States tournaments, finishing fifth or better in ten. When he returned to America in the spring of 1970 there were threats of violence from the racial activists, and in the next eleven tournaments Gary was accompanied by four armed guards. He writes: 'Those were extremely difficult days, and it was hard to remain calm and relaxed. In fact, I don't think I could have in my own strength. But through faith and prayer, instead of meeting hate with hate, I tried to respond to the ugly mood in a spirit of love and understanding. I believe the demonstrators finally came to see that they were acting against the wrong person. God gave me such a feeling of security and love that I honestly didn't feel either malice or hate toward anyone.'

Although Gary won a total of thirteen tournaments during the years 1969—1971, the other big three for another 'Majors' eluded him. His fourth Piccadilly Match Play Championship in 1971 was his major achievement. But in 1972, Gary was feeling in peak physical condition when he arrived in Birmingham, Michigan, for the 56th United States PGA Championship. Jack Nicklaus was the defending champion and a field of some of the world's finest golfers included Arnold Palmer, Lee Trevino, Billy Casper and Sam Snead. At the conclusion of the tournament, Gary emerged the winner by two strokes.

1972 was a good year: Gary went on to win another eight tournaments and approached 1973 with high expectations. His hopes were suddenly dashed, however, when he learned that he must enter hospital for major surgery. Following a long and arduous operation in February, he had many weeks of convalescence to reflect on his future prospects as a world golfer. It was not until May that he was finally cleared to return to the United States tour. During the weeks that followed, he played in seven tournaments but with miserable results. 'By July I hit bottom—the low point of my entire career. Convinced there wasn't any use going on, I headed home almost sure that my professional golf career was over.'

It was now that Gary's claim that 'faith is the most dynamic and energising force in my life' was put to the test. He believed strongly in the value of prayer and in the importance of accepting adversity, even thanking God for it. Looking back, he writes, 'when I think about those qualities which to me at least are prerequisite to success in golf, and in all of life, the one that stands out the most is the ability to accept adversity—the ability to acknowledge and handle the apparent obstacles that can, if allowed to, bring defeat . . . It is easy to be thankful for the good things that come our way in life, but it is quite another matter to thank God for the difficulties we encounter. And I do believe that success in any part of life comes only through the struggle to overcome the setbacks and hard things'.

Gary spent the next five weeks at home getting exercise and rest. Gradually his strength returned and he regained his positive outlook on life. Determined to prove himself, he flew back to the United States for a tournament in Connecticut. He finished a creditable seventh. A week later he won the Southern Open in Columbus, Georgia. From there he went on to achieve a place in the top ten in six more tournaments and, for the fifth time, won the Piccadilly World Match Play Championship in October.

1974 was a year of high drama. In April Gary won his second American Masters Championship; this immediately raised speculation about his chances of winning all four of the major tournaments in one year, the Grand Slam—a feat that had never been accomplished. The US Open Championship was played at Winged Foot Golf Club in Mamaroneck, New York, one of the toughest courses on which an Open is played. On the first day Gary led the field by one stroke. But the next day he began to slip back and finished in a tie for eighth place. His chances for a Grand Slam were doomed. It was disappointing, but Gary had long before learned that the only thing to do after losing a tournament is to forget it. 'That is what the game of life is all about: facing the adversity of defeat and then going on to the next task.'

There was some compensation when, in July, Gary took part in the 103rd British Open Championship played on the Royal Lytham and St. Annes course. Indicative of his anti-racist stance, Gary brought with him Rabbit Dyer, his regular touring caddie, the first black caddie to appear in the British Open. For three days Gary held the lead. Fifteen thousand people packed the stands as he walked to the 18th green on the final day. A difficult shot taken from up against the clubhouse wall put him back on the green just ten feet from the cup. Two putts gave him a bogey five for the hole, a two-under-par 282 for the tournament, and a win by four strokes over Peter Oosterhuis and Jack Nicklaus. 'It was my 8th major title, and the 99th overall, in pursuit of my goal of becoming the best golfer in the world.'

Recognition of his world status came on September 11, 1974, when in ceremonies held at Pinehurst, North Carolina, he was one of those inducted into the World Golf Hall of Fame. It was a high honour to be included on this first list of such outstanding golfers as Ben Hogan, Bobby Jones, Sam Snead, Gene Sarazen, Arnold Palmer and Jack Nicklaus.

In 1978, Gary reached the twenty-first year of his career as a professional golfer. Having established himself as one of the world's finest players, he might well have retired to rest on his laurels. However, he has continued to play in some of the world's major tournaments and, although not achieving the same success as in his earlier years, he has maintained a remarkably high standard of play. In 1978, when he was forty-three years old, he achieved the distinction of coming 6th in the US Open and *winning* the US Masters.

The following year he won four tournaments in South Africa, came second in the US Open and finished in the top ten of nine other major world tournaments. In 1980 Gary won the Chilean Open, the Ivory Coast Trophee Boigny and finished in the top ten of eight major international competitions.

In spite of the fact that he is now competing against many golfers half his age, Gary continues to achieve good results. In 1981 he won the South African Open for the thirteenth time—his victories spanning four decades. That year he also won the Tooth Gold Coast Classic in Australia, and finished third in the Australian Open. He won the South African PGA in 1982. Although he did not win any tournament victories in 1983, yet in 1984, he enjoyed the distinction of winning $150,000 on a single putt in the nationally televised 'Skins Game'. He tied for second place at the 66th US PGA Championship after an exciting first round of 63.

Gary attributes his success to a number of factors. He accepts St. Paul's dictum that the human body is the 'temple of God's spirit' and therefore physical fitness is essential; smoking and drinking are to be avoided as detrimental to good health. The love and support of his family are also of great importance. Gary spends much time travelling abroad but makes sure that he sees as much as possible of his wife and six children. Whatever other periods he has been able to spend at home during the year, he always reserves the *whole* month of December to spend with them at Bellerive, his ranch in the Magoebaskloof mountains north of Johannesburg. He also believes that he has done well because of hard work *and* religious faith. He says, 'In reality, faith has been the primary guideline of my life. But when I'm playing a tournament, I don't *pray* to win. Probably most of the players are doing that! After all, there can be only one winner, and there's no special reason why God should pick me to win. Rather, I pray for courage, strength, and guidance, and the ability to go on loving *everyone*. Winning is not the final measure of success. That is really determined by the type of person you are . . . the quality of life you live.

'The pressures of the golfing circuit on a tournament player are great and this is why I endeavour to walk hand in hand with the Lord in my daily life, and fully realise that without this wonderful contact I would not have that inner peace which is so important. No matter where I am, I can commune with Him about everything and I am able to turn to Him for the necessary comfort of soul and spirit.'

Gary feels convinced that God has a part for him to play

in life as a professional golfer. This includes 'being an ambassador of goodwill and spreading feelings of love and peace wherever I go—in the galleries, along the fairways and greens, in hotel lobbies, everywhere. It is my prayer that God will use me to mirror His love and goodwill in every part of my personal and professional life. I really feel I'm a salesman for God when I travel. I am sure of our basic needs are the same. That is why I recommend Jesus Christ as the only one who can answer your needs and give you "The peace of God that passes all understanding".'

For further reading:

Gary Player—World Golfer: with Floyd Thatcher, Word Books: 1974

4: Serving for God

Stan Smith: Tennis Champion

<u>Born 14 December 1946</u>

Even at three in the morning, it was stifling travelling home from Colorado during the August heat wave. Eleven year-old Stan Smith was asleep in the back of the van. His sixteen year-old brother, Steve, recently licensed as a driver, gripped the wheel tighter and took deep breaths in an effort to keep awake. But it was of no avail. Momentarily he dozed off; the van swerved, rolled over and crashed on the grassy strip between the traffic lanes. The rear doors flew open and Stan was hurled through the air, landing thirty feet away in a patch of weeds. He tried to wipe what he thought was sweat from his head and found his hand covered in blood. It felt as though his head was smashed and one knee crushed. At least he was alive, but his life was so full of activity that so serious an accident filled him with apprehension about the future; he lay there wondering if he would ever be able to walk and run again.

Stan was the youngest of three boys. His father was a physical education teacher in Pasadena, California. All the family were fine athletes and although no one pressurised Stan into sport, it was natural that as he grew up he came to enjoy skiing, high jumping, playing basketball, football and tennis. In addition, his mother made sure that he learned, somewhat unwillingly, to play the piano. He also had to attend Sunday School fairly regularly, sometimes staying for the church service that followed, although at the time it meant little to him.

His injuries were not as bad as he had feared, and after a few weeks in a wheelchair, Stan was discharged from hospital and was able to take up his various sporting interests again. He and a group of friends decided to take tennis lessons at the public courts in Pasadena. Stan began to feel an enthusiasm for the game, and a group of parents formed the 'Pasadena Tennis Patrons', an organisation to help their boys and girls to learn to play properly. They hired Pancho Segura to be instructor at Saturday 'clinics'. These five-hour sessions commenced with warming up exercises and went on to a series of drills to practise service and stroke play.

During his senior year at school, Stan had to make the first major decision of his life—whether to devote himself to basketball or tennis. Being tall and having an unusually long reach, he had done well playing for the Pasadena High School and the school coach wanted him to go on to play basketball at university level. But in the Autumn of 1963, he went to his coach and said, 'I'd really like to become a good *tennis* player; so I'm going to drop basketball'.

Having committed himself to tennis, Stan now augmented his Saturdays at the Patrons' clinics with five-hour sessions at the Los Angeles Tennis Club. Full of enthusiasm, he applied to be a ball boy during the 1963 Davis Cup matches between Mexico and the U.S., held at Los Angeles. He was turned down because it was feared he would trip over his size-thirteen tennis shoes! However, he was gradually overcoming his youthful clumsiness and his rapid improvement on the court surprised many of his friends. By the Spring of 1964, he was ranked seventh among the juniors in Southern California, and he confided in his current girl friend that he had set himself four major goals in tennis. 'My first goal is to be in the Davis Cup team that will go to Australia and win back the Cup for America. The second goal is to become the No. 1 player in the U.S. Third is to win Wimbledon. Fourth is to become the best player in the world.'

Although he was offered a scholarship to go to the University of California at Los Angeles, he had set his sights on going to the University of Southern California (USC).

He continued to improve and won the Ojai Valley Inter-scholastic singles title by beating two fine players, Steve Tidball and Tom Karp. Although beaten by Bob Lutz in the final of the Southern California championships, he was offered a scholarship to his first choice of university, the USC.

Soon after leaving high school, Stan took part in the National Hard Court championships for juniors. Although he was not seeded, he won his way through to the final and took the singles title. He then went on his first major trip as part of a four-player group sent by the Southern California Tennis Association to compete in three national junior tournaments; his successes included beating the talented Bob Lutz. The big event of the season was the 18–and-under national championships in Kalamazoo. For most of the young competitors, this was the equivalent of England's Wimbledon and the nervous strain was considerable. For many of them, winning was so important that the game was no longer fun, whereas Stan, the newcomer, felt little pressure and was able to enjoy himself thoroughly. With a measure of good fortune, he reached the finals and defeated Billy Harris, a player who had previously dominated junior tennis, and took the national title. Stan attributed his sudden rise to success partly to his very strict training programme and endless practice, and partly to the coaching of Segura, who had taught him the finesse of tennis—not *how* to hit the ball, but *when* and *where*.

With the financial help of the Patrons, Stan, now nine-teen, flew to London to try to qualify for the 1966 All England Championships at Wimbledon. His national junior titles were not sufficient to qualify him for automatic entry. Consequently, he had to compete in preliminary rounds against sixty-three other hopefuls at Roehampton for the eight remaining places at Wimbledon. He won his first match and lost the next, but gained access to the tournament by being drawn as one of the 'Lucky Losers' to replace one of the 128 competitors for the singles who dropped out at the last minute. On the same day he qualified with Steve Tidball for the Wimbledon doubles. Stan's opponent in the first round of the singles was a little known Dutchman whom he defeated, only to be eliminated in the next round by the formidable Rafael Osuna of Mexico. In the doubles, he and his partner were drawn against Roy Emerson and Fred Stolle, the No. 1 seeds—a match in which they were soundly defeated!

At the university of Southern California, Stan shared a room with Jim Marsh, an outstanding basketball player. He was surprised to find that Jim read his Bible every night. By his second year, Stan had come to respect the sincerity of his room-mate's Christian convictions. He noticed that those students who seemed to have a more balanced approach to life than others and a happier outlook were often strong Christians. Some of them shared their faith with him and this had a profound effect on Stan: 'Tennis had become so much a part of my life that I had never thought about a deeper meaning for my existence and had never considered what I would do if I could no longer play tennis'.

In his brief autobiography, *It's More Than Just a Game*, Stan says, 'Off and on, I kept asking Jim Marsh questions about his faith and the Bible. I also went to a few meetings with other USC athletes who were Christians. Then, one day when I was in my room in the dorm, I felt I had heard all I had to hear, that I could keep inventing excuses and finding questions forever, and that it was time to honestly consider all that I had found out about Christ. This I did, and right there, in my own quiet way, I asked God to come into my life. No, there were no lightening bolts, no loud sirens. Just quiet. Peace. There was assurance that Christ loved me, that God was sovereign, and that He could and would be with me all the days of my life, to share my joy, to provide strength when needed most.' Stan began to attend a fellowship group of university athletes. Already he could see that athletes particularly could have a widespread influence on student life. Studying the Bible and discussing his new-found faith, Stan became convinced that God had a plan for his life, as for *every* other individual.

In his second year, he started as the University's No. 2 player and by the end of the season was No. 1. At the National Collegiate tournament during his junior year, he lost in the quarter-finals of the singles, but teamed up with Bob Lutz to win the doubles and thereby help USC to retain the overall championship.

Although much of college life revolved around tennis, Stan became very involved in the 'Big Brothers of America', an organisation that works with fatherless boys on a one-to-one basis. He recruited eleven other students and each was assigned a boy in the nine-to-twelve age range. They tried to meet the boys individually once a week and in addition went on group outings—swimming, fishing and playing team games.

During his senior year, Stan beat his old rival, Bob Lutz, to take the singles title at the National Collegiate Athletic Association tournament at Trinity College in Texas. Then, *partnered* by Lutz, he went on to win the doubles; USC also retained the team title. In April, 1968, he and Lutz were chosen to represent the United States of America as the doubles pair in the Davis Cup, and won their game in three sets. A further series of doubles victories culminated in success at the British indoor championships where, partnered by Bob Lutz, he won the men's doubles and, with Margaret Court of Australia, won the mixed doubles. Stan and Bob were also in the US team which went to Australia in late December for the final round of the Davis Cup competition. This was the fulfilment of the first of his four goals. They went on court for their doubles match knowing they could clinch the victory for the US. This they did, winning 6–4, 6–4, 6–2. After the Davis Cup triumph, Stan took another major step forward in Melbourne when he defeated Arthur Ashe, the world's No. 1 amateur at the time.

During the final Challenge Round of the Davis Cup in 1969, Stan had his first opportunity to play Davis Cup *singles* and beat the brilliant Romanian, Ion Tiriac 6–8, 6–3, 5–7, 6–4, 6–4. Then he combined with Lutz against Tiriac and Ilie Nastase to win the doubles in five sets and to give the US an unassailable 3–0 lead.

In his singles match against Nastase, Stan won a more personal victory. In was a long, exhausing match. Nastase won the first two sets and Stan the next two. In the final set they were 9–all and Nastase now began his notorious fast-slow-fast type of game to frustrate and irritate his opponent. As a result, Stan missed two easy shots, and, feeling sick and discouraged, was on the point of hurling his racket at the ground, his confidence gone. In the brief interval between games, he sat and reflected on his life as a Christian. He remembers, 'I asked myself the question: Did I really want God to run my life or was I going to do it myself? The answer was I had forgotten Him and was letting my own childish self and temper control me. As a follower of Christ, I knew this was wrong. I knew He wouldn't care much whether I won or lost, but whether I was reflecting Him and playing the way I had trained myself to play. My frustration seemed to drain away. I was confident again. In the nineteenth game of that final set, I broke Nastase's serve and went on to win the match. The victory over Nastase wasn't nearly as important as the victory Christ helped me to win over myself.'

By the end of the year, Stan had reached the finals of nine major tournaments, of which he had won eight. As a result, he was ranked No. 1 player in the US in 1969. Having helped to recapture the Davis Cup the previous year, he had now attained half of the improbable goals he had set himself in 1964. 'All this success gave me a heady feeling. Like a lot of others, I was tempted to think I was accomplishing all these things on my own. Dealing with success, I found, is not easy. But I learned that this situation, like all others, could be put into proper perspective by turning to the Lord, talking matters over with Him and offering thanks for everything. I know that whatever successes I have had I owe to God, and it is a pleasure to know that He has been helping me. And it is a relief to know that I am not out there trying to accomplish these deeds on my own.'

Early in 1970, an unfortunate injury forced Stan to cancel several tournaments and exhibitions. It happened when Lutz, Tiriac, Ralston, Nastase and Stan were walking back from practice. Nastase came up behind Tiriac and playfully tripped him, pretending that Stan was responsible. Tiriac chased Stan, caught him and, in fun, threw him on the grass. Stan, who was carrying four rackets under his arm, strained his right shoulder muscles, producing intense pain, and forcing him to withdraw from the competition. After undergoing treatment for several weeks without making any real progress, he was introduced to a doctor who was experimenting with cortisone injections. Following concentrated treatment he advised Stan: 'Go to England. Practise for Wimbledon and play hard'. Stan followed his advice and was delighted to reach the quarter-finals. A few weeks later he was able to play in the Davis Cup Challenge Round against West Germany in Cleveland. For the third successive year, he and Lutz earned the third and decisive point for the US by winning the doubles.

Over-confidence prevented Stan becoming the US No. 1 player in 1970. Cliff Richey was the other contender in the deciding match and the final set went on into a tie breaker which either of them could win by one point. During the final rally, Stan hit the ball down his opponent's side line; thinking Richey would not reach it, he took his racket out of his right hand ready to shake hands with Cliff. But Richey took a flying lunge and a wild swing, and hit the ball back off the top of his racket. Stan saw the ball coming over the net and made a desperate attempt to hit it, but was too late. Richey won and on the outcome of that match he was ranked US No. 1. Another bitter setback followed when Stan was serving with match point in his favour against Pancho Gonzales, and still failed to win the match. There was, however, some compensation. While still in London, Stan partnered Ken Rosewall and won the

Wembley doubles. This was followed by a victory in Stockholm when Stan beat Rosewall in the semi-final and Ashe in the final and, with Lutz, also took the doubles.

Stan celebrated his twenty-fourth birthday in Tokyo by winning the Grand Prix Masters against Rosewall and by receiving the same day his final army draft notice instructing him to report for induction in Pasadena on 16th December.

He was posted to Fort Ord, California for basic training. Although he did not receive any specially favourable treatment during training, much of his time in the Army was spent in organising tennis clinics for the military personnel. He was also permitted to represent the US in Davis Cup matches and to enter other tennis competitions as preparation. Over-confidence again lost him a vital tournament at Wimbledon in 1971. Having defeated Tom Gorman in the semi-final, he played John Newcombe, the defending champion, in the final and went into the lead with two sets to one. 'During the fourth set, my mind wandered badly. I actually became preoccupied with thoughts about what I would say in my speech and what tune I would ask to have played at the Wimbledon ball that night.' At that moment, Newcombe had a heavy fall and pretended to be badly hurt, drawing a laugh from the crowd. With his concentration broken, Stan's game fell apart. He lost his next service game and dropped the set. In the fifth set, with the game two all, he double-faulted twice in succession, then mis-hit an easy volley. Newcombe won the set 6–4 and so became Men's Singles Champion.

However, 1971 brought two important victories. First, Stan beat Jan Kodes of Czechoslovakia to win the US Open at Forest Hills then, for the fourth year running, helped the US to win the deciding Davis Cup point.

At Wimbledon in 1972, Stan again reached the final. His match against Nastase was timed for 2 p.m. on Saturday, but it poured with rain the whole afternoon and it was announced that the game would be postponed to Sunday. That evening, a minister spoke to him on the 'phone, asking him not to compromise his standards by playing on Sunday.

Stan replied, 'Back in the US we have athletes, some of them fine Christians, who are often required to compete on Sundays. To me, the important thing is to have a close relationship with God *every* day of the week and to do His will. I don't think it will be a disappointment to God if I play on Sunday, because He has given me whatever talent I have and I think He expects me to put it to use.'

Sunday came and Nastase took the opening set 6–4. Stan took the next two 6–3, 6–3 and then lost the fourth set 4–6. In the fifth set, Nastase saved two match points and tied at 5–5. Stan held his serve to make it 6–5 and then Nastase went to 40–love. Thinking he had lost the game, Stan hit the ball as hard as he could without worrying whether it was in or out. It was in, and he hit two more winners, Nastase double-faulted, and it was Stan's advantage for match point. As Nastase went for a backhand shot, a young girl spectator let out a loud 'Ooohhh'. Nastase was momentarily distracted as he went for the ball, his return hit the top of the net tape and fell on his side. Stan looked at Nastase, thinking they would have to play a let because of the distraction, but there was no call, and Stan leaped the net to give Nastase a winner's consoling handshake. He had fulfilled his third goal. In addition, at the end of the year Stan shared with John Newcombe the Martini and Rossi Golden Racquet for being voted the top player in the world. He would have preferred being the outright No. 1.

In 1972, in the revised Davis Cup Challenge Round system, the US team met Romania in the final round. It was the first time the finals has been held in Eastern Europe. It was a match full of political tension and national fervour, played on clay by the choice of the host nation. Stan's fiancée, Margie, wrote an encouraging letter which Stan shared with the team captain, Dennis Ralston—another player whose life was already being changed through the influence of Stan and other Christian friends. The letter said, 'You are representing the US and Christ, and it won't be as important for you to win the matches as it will be for you to represent the Lord well to all those people around the world who will be seeing the competition'.

In the second match, between Tiriac and Gorman, trouble flared up when Enrique Moren, the neutral referee from Argentina, changed several of the linesmen's calls. Stan was keenly aware of the explosive atmosphere when he went on court to play Tiriac in the fourth match. Stan felt as though he were up against all Tiriac's relatives, neighbours and ancestors, and, worst of all, the line judges. With the sets at 1–1, Tiriac served very wide. However, one of the linesmen ruled that the ball had landed inside the line. Stan looked at the line judge but he turned away; Stan pointed to the mark left by the ball six inches *outside* the line, but the judge refused to change his call. Another equally bad decision drove Stan near to despair. He looked across at Ralston—who had been praying that *he* might keep calm. Stan was reassured to see that he was still ice cool and not about to explode with rage as he might have done a few months earlier. 'Without saying a word or without changing his expression, Dennis seemed to be saying to me, "Well, this is what we expected. We've got to put up with it. Take it easy. Don't let this stuff bother you. Remember out goal." I can truly say that having talked and prayed with Dennis about coping with such a situation helped immeasurably. It was comforting to see the new Ralston so much in command of himself and the situation, and it was strengthening to recall our goal was, above all, to be worthy representatives of Christ and country.'

Some more dubious calls went against the American, but he still took the set 6–4. The Romanian fans redoubled their cheering for their national hero, 'Teer-ree-ack, Teer-ree-ack', and the Romanian took the next set 6–2. 'At that point, I closed my eyes and prayed, "Please, Lord, give me the strength to handle this situation. Don't let me get so upset that I can't play my best". Stan commenced the fifth set with an ace down the middle and playing to the full extent of his ability served a further three aces to win the set 6–0. In consequence, the American team went on to win the Cup. Looking back, Dennis Ralston comments: 'There is no player on earth who could have won that match other than Stan Smith, and the reason he could win was because he had this strong faith which coloured his whole attitude to life and to what he was doing—he believed that the Lord was working in his life. It was a real witness to me that he could keep that calm under those trying conditions.'

Primarily as a result of his controlled behaviour in that match, Stan was awarded the Fair Play Trophy in 1972. In addition, he was again awarded the Martini and Rossi Gold Racquet as the No. 1 player in the world, and this time he was the sole nominee. He had achieved the last of his four goals.

Stan was discharged from the Army late in 1972 and joined the World Championship Tennis circuit early in 1973. Some critics had argued that Stan should not have received the Gold Racquet award as he had not faced all the best players, some of whom were contract professionals. Stan set himself a new goal—to win the W.C.T. singles title in his first year on the professional circuit. At the end of the season, the players with the best records met for the W.C.T. championships. First, Stan and Lutz won the doubles in Montreal, Canada. Then at Dallas, Stan fought out the singles with the world's top professionals. Things went so well for him in his opening match, against Alexander, that at one point a spectator shouted to him, 'Cut out the miracles and start playing tennis!' Stan was in peak form and having beaten Rod Laver went into the finals against Arthur Ashe, whom he defeated 6–3, 6–3, 4–6, 6–4. He had now proved to everyone's satisfaction that he *was* the world's top player.

The following year, Stan received the worst setback of his career. In an attempt to improve his second serve he changed to a heavier racquet. As a result, he developed a very sore fore-arm which, later, was found to be the product of torn tendons in his elbow. This led to the sensation of the former champion being eliminated in the first round of the 1974 Wimbledon tournament by Byron Bertram of South Africa, 6–1, 6–2, 6–1. Numerous forms of treatment failed to cure the continuing pain and stiffness in the injured arm. For the next three years Stan was unable to play at his best. From being the world's number one player, he now found himself struggling to maintain any sort of form in major tournaments. It was a severe test of his faith to cope with the frustrations of mediocre performance and poor results. However, it was during this injury-plagued period of decline that he wrote, 'This is something I have prayed about and have asked the Lord to help me overcome. One of the most comforting realisations is that I am convinced all of this is part of God's plan for my life. He has cared for me so marvelously throughout my life and I know he is still guiding me'.

It took many months of therapy and a programme of weight training to strengthen his arm muscles before Stan could begin his classic come-back. His performance in 1978 included some outstanding efforts—the losing finalist to Jimmy Connors at Denver and Beckenham, a strong semi-final match against Bjorn Borg in the Ramazotti Cup and, in the late summer, he won the Atlanta Journal-Constitution Open.

Positive proof of his return to form came in 1979 when, in singles, he beat Ilie Nastase to win the Gray International Open in Cleveland, Ohio, and won the Fischer Grand Prix in Vienna, defeating Wotjek Fibak. Partnered by Bob Lutz he won three important doubles championships in the US and, with Gene Mayer, took the European Indoor Open at Cologne.

In 1980, again partnered by Lutz, Stan won the Alan/King Caesars Palace Tennis Classic In Las Vegas. He also won both the Frankfurt Indoor Singles Championship and, with Vijay Amritraj, the doubles. There were several other highlights in the season. Stan and Lutz fought their way through to the Final of the Doubles at Wimbledon, only to be beaten in an exciting match by Peter McNamara and Paul McNamee of Australia. Partnered by Amritraj, stan won the ABN World Tennis Tournament at Rotterdam, and went on to win the US Open Doubles Championship, defeating John McEnroe and Peter Fleming. He finished the season rated individually No. 1 in the Grand Prix Doubles standings.

In 1981 Stan and Lutz again reached the Final of the Doubles at Wimbledon. In a closely contested match, they were beaten 6–4, 6–4, 6–4 by McEnroe and Fleming. In the Singles, Stan caused a sensation by taking the second set from the much younger McEnroe, although eventually losing the match 7–5, 3–6, 6–1, 6–2; McEnroe went on to win the Championship.

Stan's contribution to tennis is not limited to his on-court performances. One of the founders of the men's players union, the Association of Tennis Professionals (ATP), he served on its board of directors from 1972–79 and is a past treasurer. With Margie, his wife—whom he married in November 1974—he also serves as the ATP liaison with the Cystic Fibrosis Society. His philanthropic work has earned him the ATP-Adidas Sportsmanship Award in 1978 and the ATP Service Award in 1979. He has also been awarded an honorary doctorate in humane letters from Greenville College in Illinois for his work as a representative of the US and for his effectiveness as a Christian advocate.

His standing as a world-class tennis player has given Stan many different opportunities to speak about his Christian Faith. He is active in numerous Christian organisations and fellowships and a quietly persuasive speaker at various meetings—particularly of businessmen, fellow sportsmen and groups of young people. House-parties are another effective means of outreach. The practice is for a couple to host a dinner to which friends and neighbours are invited. Stan, and perhaps one or two others, go along to give their testimony after the meal and to share in personal counselling.

Stan feels that his faith has grown and his spiritual life has been extended by being able to stay with Christian families when on tour. A devoted family man, whenever possible he likes to be accompanied by his wife and young son. He says, 'On the professional circuit one has to be aware continually of the priorities of one's life. I try to have God first, family second, friends third and my profession fourth. Sometimes number four tends to jump up over the other three and when that happens my life will rise and fall with my wins and losses, making it hard on me and harder on Margie. However, having children has helped us to realise the priorities more realistically as we travel the "jet-set" tennis circuit.'

The family resides at Sea Pines Plantation, Hilton Head Island, Southern California, where Stan serves as a touring professional. He is currently broadcasting a tennis spot on local radio and has been engaged to do commentary on tournaments for 'US Cablevision', the largest cable network in the US. He says, 'I've always been goal-oriented. New challenges on and off the court are the things that motivate me the most now. You can't live in the past.'

Stan Smith has been paid the compliment of being called 'the tennis player's tennis player'. He has represented the United States twelve times in the Davis Cup. His total of twenty-six US men's singles and doubles titles is second only to Bill Tilden. Stan and Bob Lutz are the only doubles team in tennis history to win US national titles on all four surfaces—grass, clay, hardcourt and indoor.

He hopes to go on playing as long as health permits. In this respect he feels that his lingering elbow injury has led to the deepening of his faith and a more philosophic outlook on life. In his book, *It's More Than Just A Game* he says, 'During these times of injuries, or just a temporary lack of confidence, I have tried to remember that Romans 8: 28 says, ". . . all things work together for good for them that love God, to them who are the called according to his purpose." Oftentimes in my life and in the lives of others, I've seen that the difficult situations of today have actually been God's way of placing the final stepping-stones for the blessings of tomorrow. Even though it is still hard to accept these trying times, when I look back on them, I can see

God working through these experiences in an exciting and dynamic way . . . I am sure that all these things that have come my way have been God's way of showing His love towards me as He works His plan for my life.'

For further reading:

It's More Than Just A Game: Flemming H. Revell Co., 1977. Marshall, Morgan and Scott, 1978.

5: The Nelson Touch

Larry Nelson: Champion Golfer

Born 10 September 1947

At 5.30pm, local time, the second storm of the week burst over the Oakmont Country Club golf course near Pittsburgh. Brilliant forked lightning, crashing thunder and rain that saturated the greens in minutes sent the crowd scurrying for cover. It could hardly have come at a worse moment for Larry Nelson. The 1983 US Open Golf Championship was approaching its climax, at last Larry was playing well and he had no wish to break off when victory was within his grasp. Earlier in the tournament no one would have given him a chance. But, gradually he had caught up with the leaders until now, at the fourteenth hole, he had levelled with Tom Watson, the previous year's winner. When the siren sounded signalling the suspension of play, Watson quickly left the course, but Larry braved the elements long enough to putt the fifteenth hole, before reluctantly making for the club-house. Later, when asked why he had risked carrying on playing in the lightning, Larry replied, 'If I had been hit, I knew where I was going'. He, and the five other competitors who had not completed the final round, now had another fourteen hours to wait before they could continue.

The next morning was heavy and overcast. The siren sounded at 10 o'clock to signal the resumption of play. Larry took a club from his caddie and stood contemplating his tee shot to the sixteenth green. He was conscious of an awesome silence. He addressed the ball. It was not one of his best shots. But six minutes later he holed the sixteenth with a gigantic sixty foot putt for a birdie which took him into the lead. There were no problems at the seventeenth. At the eighteenth, Larry's drive carried the ball to the edge of the green, but it took him three putts to complete the hole. Then he returned to the scorer's tent to see what Watson would do. Although the defending champion finished in style with a thirty-five foot putt, overall he had taken one stroke more than Larry. The amiable Georgian from Atlanta had achieved the greatest victory of his ten-year career as a professional golfer.

Larry is five feet nine inches tall, a golfer who relies on touch and finesse rather than sledge-hammer blows with the big clubs. 'His voice is Southern and soft, his manner is warm and courtly and a sense of humour flickers constantly in the background of his conversation,' writes John Hopkins of the *Sunday Times*. Unlike most professionals, Larry had hardly touched a golf club until he was twenty-one. But as he grew up, he had shown a natural aptitude for all ball games. He was brought up by his father to believe that if he worked hard enough and had faith in what he was doing, he could be as good as anyone. At high school he proved himself a promising baseball and basketball player. He attended the Southern Technical College for a year on an athletic scholarship and had high hopes of becoming a professional baseball pitcher.

Larry left college in 1968, at the time of the Vietnam war and he was immediately drafted into the Army. He spent the next eighteen months as an artillery observer with the light infantry in the paddy fields and jungles of South-East Asia. 'I was stationed with a guy who talked a lot about golf and it was he who first got me interested in the game,' Larry recalls.

Three days after his discharge from the Army, an incident occurred which was to change the direction of Larry's life. He went out and spent a day pitching on the baseball mound. He was badly out of practice and, as a result, injured his pitching arm so seriously that the doctors advised him he would never be able to pitch professionally. It was a staggering blow to his sporting ambition.

Meanwhile, Larry had obtained a job as an illustrator at the Lockheed Aircraft Company. One evening, with time to spare, he wandered into a golf driving range. Although his interest had been aroused by the enthusiasm of his army friend, until then he had never seriously considered playing. He took a bucket of balls and tried a few tentative swings. Soon he was hitting his shots straight and hard. To his surprise, he found he thoroughly enjoyed the experience.

Larry began to practise regularly and gradually the idea dawned that maybe he could make his name at golf instead of baseball. To help improve his strokes, Larry studied Ben Hogan's book, *Modern Fundamentals of Golf*. 'Ben said you can learn all the mechanics in six or eight months,' Larry recalls, 'after that it is just a matter of mental application.' He always carried the book with him and set out to model his game on that of its author, one of the super-stars of golf.

Larry became so enthusiastic about his new-found sport that he gave up his job at Lockheed's and went to work as an assistant to the professional at Pine Tree Golf Club in Kennesow. Apart from working in the club shop, Larry set goals for himself out on the course. 'I gave myself three months to break 40 strokes for nine holes. I made it with a 37. Next I aimed to shoot par for 18 holes, and then under par.' He reached both goals less than a year after he started playing. During the next two years he entered as many tournaments as time permitted and his play continued to improve under the supervision of Bert Seagraves, the club professional.

His early efforts were unspectacular but he persisted and his first taste of success came in the Florida State Open in 1973. He lost by a shot, but as a result he was granted the PGA Card which enabled him to compete on the professional tournament circuit. He now had to face some of the world's finest golfers such as Jack Nicklaus, Tom Watson, Lee Trevino and Arnold Palmer. After eleven tournaments as a professional he had earned only $325. 'I was in awe of everybody who had more experience,' Larry says. But, gradually, he overcame his diffidence and realised he could compete with anyone, even if he had to wait for success. The next three years brought improved results and higher earnings, but still no outright win.

One day in 1976, Larry and his wife, Gayle, were on their way to the Bob Hope Desert Classic. As they were driving through California there was a blinding dust storm. Suddenly their car was hit from behind by a large, speeding truck. Larry was slightly injured and had to withdraw from the tournament. However, the accident prompted him to renew a spiritual search that had begun two years earlier when he and Gayle had attended an evening Bible study held for the professionals on tour. That night the speaker was Billy Graham. Larry felt as though the famous evangelist was speaking directly to him about his relationship with God. He had been brought up in a Christian home and had continued attending church whenever he could. But, as Dr. Graham spoke, he realised that simply going to church does not necessarily make one a Christian. He began to question inwardly whether he had ever actually committed his life to Jesus Christ.

Billy Graham finished with some practical advice: 'If you really want to know God and have Him direct your life, read the Bible, particularly the Book of John and the Letter to the Romans.' Larry had tried reading the Bible before, but having started at the very beginning, he had given up before completing Genesis. He did not forget what the evangelist had said, but, at the time, he was too occupied with golf to act on his advice.

Early in 1975, Gayle told Larry that she had asked Christ to guide her life and to be her personal Saviour. He was very surprised, but over the next few weeks he saw that the change in her life was real. 'She was more aware of my feelings and needs, for example. There was something different about her, a change hard to explain,' Larry recollects. 'She didn't come at me to make the same decision; but there was a quiet peace about her—and it lasted. It was hard for me to get over that she had admitted there was sin in her life. I figured that if Gayle had sin in her life, I had a lot more. I, too, needed God's forgiveness.'

Waiting for the next tournament at a motel in San Diego, Larry picked up a book from the night-stand entitled, *Love*. It was a copy of the New Testament in modern English. Remembering Billy Graham's words about coming to know God, he began to read St. John's gospel and Paul's letter to the Romans. 'Reading that,' says Larry, 'I came to realise that I was separated from God because of my sin, and I was convicted of that sin. Yet because God loved me and demonstrated his love by sending His Son to die for me on the Cross, I knew that all I had to do was to ask God to forgive me and to come into my life. So that's what I did there in our motel room in San Diego. It wasn't dramatic with lights flashing or bells ringing, but there was a peace and assurance that I was a child of God and if I died that night I would go to heaven and be with Him eternally.'

Although able to hold his own on the tournament trail, by 1979 Larry had still no major US victory to his credit. Then, at last, he had a taste of real success. Battling against gusting winds, he gained his first tournament victory, the Jackie Gleason-Inverrary Classic played in Florida. Then he was runner-up in the Danny Thomas Memphis Classic when Gil Morgan won a play-off at the second extra hole. A week later he was in Illinois to win the Western Open in a play-off with Ben Crenshaw.

Larry finished in the top three in the next six tournaments in which he competed. These results included a tie for second in the World Series and an equal fourth in the US Open. He was also selected for his first Ryder Cup match, an international competition between the United States and Europe. He was paired with Lanny Wadkins and together they won their four doubles matches. On the last day, Larry defeated Severiano Ballesteros of Spain in an exciting singles match to help his team win the encounter. At the end of the year, Larry wound up second only to Tom Watson in the PGA Money Winners' List—a sure indication of his overall success. This was an astonishing feat for someone who had been playing golf for only ten years.

People began asking Larry if being a Christian had improved his golf. He replied that, 'there are a lot of really good golfers who are not committed to Jesus Christ, but I feel that I am a better person because I know Him and have more effect on the people around me because of my faith'. Asked if he prayed to win, Larry said that he 'never prays during a round to get a difficult iron on to the green or a tricky putt into the hole—that is not what religion is about'. Rather, he prays for peace of mind to enable him to play to the best of his ability all the time.

Although a back injury caused Larry to slump in the second half of 1982, he won the Atlantic Classic and still achieved eleventh place on the PGA Money List. The following year saw him win the Greater Greensboro Open and repeat his previous Ryder Cup success by gaining 4 wins in 4 matches. But it was the 1981 PGA Championship held in August on the bright green fairways of the Atlantic Athletic Club which was the highlight of his year. Larry was playing on his local course, as he then lived nearby at Acworth. On the Sunday morning, before playing the final round, he attended his own church. He was amused—and enheartened by the hymns in the service. They included 'Victory in Jesus', and 'The old rugged cross' which has the line 'Till my trophies at last I lay down'! With five holes to go, Fuzzy Zoeller trailed Larry by five strokes. But then Larry was in trouble. Two poor shots had left him struggling on the par-four fourteenth hole, requiring an extraordinary pitch shot. He steadied himself, stroked the ball and saw it roll safely towards the cup. Soon after, he parred the final hole to win by four strokes. It was his first *major* tournament win and he was his home-town's hero.

When Larry committed himself to Christ, he became an active member of the Golf Tour Bible Study—a group which meets regularly on the US tournament circuit. Larry reckons there are some twenty to thirty pros, together with their wives, who are interested enough to attend. He also began sharing his faith with church and civic groups. Larry comments, 'Even though public speaking still scares me to death, I think it is important to share my faith whenever possible'. He became active with the 'Fellowship of Christian Athletes' (FCA) taking part in numerous FCA professional—amateur tournaments and serving as a leader at several FCA Junior Golf Conferences. His involvement was recognised in 1981 when he was named the organisation's 'Pro Athlete of the Year'. Larry compares golf to everyday life. 'We have bad breaks and good breaks, but we are supposed to do the best we possibly can with what God has given us,' he says. 'We golfers must acknowledge that God has given us the ability to play golf and to do so for His Glory.'

This faith undergirds Larry's determination and refusal to be daunted by the 'bad breaks'. After slipping to twenty-first on the US Order of Merit in 1982 he had been so off-form that in mid season 1983 he was a lowly ninety-second on the all-important Money List. But then came the US open. At the half-way stage he was seven shots behind the leaders, but then proceeded to play the final thirty-nine holes to win with an amazing ten under par. Larry was unable to win any major tournaments in 1984 until October when he suddenly found form to win the Walt Disney World at lake Buena Vista by one stroke from Hubert Green.

The US Open is his most prestigious win to date. Undoubtedly, there will be more to come. Even when he is not winning major trophies, Larry is a consistently good player. He has a 100% record in the Ryder Cup—a unique feat among contemporary players.

John Hopkins of the *Sunday Times* describes Larry: 'Nelson's pleasingly-shaped face is unlined, and bears so few signs of wear and tear from the thousands of short putts he has had to hole that he doesn't look anything like his age. His voice is southern and soft, his manner is warm and courtly and a sense of humour flickers constantly in the background of his conversation.' Peter Ryde of *The*

Times says of him: 'Nelson is quiet and small, but he is neither withdrawn nor cocky. He likes to mix with people and enjoys pro-ams because, in the best American tradition, he believes he owes something to those he meets, most of whom are supporting the tournaments.'

Larry believes that it is essential to get one's priorities in life right. In an interview with Dave Bell for the magazine *The Christian Athlete*, he lists three major priorities, his faith, his family and his job. 'My first priority is God . . . to seek him, to do things that please him and bring glory to him. I need to return thanks for his blessings. Regular Bible study, prayer and fellowship with other Christians have been the key to my spiritual growth. The closer my relationship with God, the smoother and more consistent my life becomes.'

'One thing a pro golfer doesn't have much of is time. I have a wonderful wife Gayle and two boys I love very much. It's sometimes difficult to pass up a lucrative tournament or appearance to be with them, but ultimately there's no comparison as to which is more important.'

'At the beginning of each year I sit down and determine my tournament participation and other commitments. Then I consider other invitations I've received to earn extra income through appearances, pro-am tournaments, etc. When possible I schedule blocks of time at home with my family. It's important I make them a priority in my scheduling.'

'Defining the job of a pro golfer is hard. It's like someone who owns a business . . . so much of the person is wrapped up in their job that it's difficult to separate one from the other. For instance, my appearances and speaking engagements don't directly involve golf but they're all part of being a pro golfer. Since they can eat up a tremendous amount of time you have to be selective.'

All Christians sometimes become low spiritually. Larry's remedy is to 'go back to basics'. He says, 'The basics in my life are that God loves me, has a plan for my life, cares for me personally and understands my troubles, wants and needs.'

'Professional athletes are in a field that makes it extremely difficult to keep priorities straight. Everything is performance orientated. That's why I need my faith. Golf can provide many things materially but only the Lord can give me joy, peace and life eternal regardless of my performance on the course.'

6: 'Jesus Saves'

Alex Ribeiro: Racing Driver

Born 7 November 1948

Thirty-five entrants lined up for the start of the 1978 Eifel-rennen Formula Two* motor race at Germany's legendary Nurburgring. The drivers revved their engines to a screaming crescendo of sound as they waited for the starter's flag to drop. The brightly painted cars each bore the decals of their sponsors—everything from motor oil to perfume. On the front row of the grid one car stood out: Alex Ribeiro's vivid red Hart-powered March simply carried the emblem *Jesus Saves*. Round the track, among the advertisements on the crash barriers, were banners with the same crisp message.

It was a race that will be talked about for years to come. At the start Ribeiro shot away into the lead, but very soon there were five cars fighting wheel to wheel, and any one of them might have taken this third round of the European Formula Two Championship.

After an hour of breathtaking driving, the race was between Ribeiro's March-Hart, the Chevron-Hart of Keke Rosberg—who had already shattered the lap record—and Eddie Cheever's March-BMW. With three laps to go, Riberio and Cheever hurtled down the straight side by side, and went into the chicane* with their wheels interlocked. Ribeiro edged ahead and Rosberg took up the challenge.

*International formula using 2–litre racing engines of any origin.

*Artificial bend to slow cars.

On the last lap Ribeiro pulled out coming in to the straight, and although Rosberg was able to close up in the tow, Ribeiro managed to get into the chicane first. Rosberg braked at the last possible moment, closing the gap, but it was too late, and Ribeiro lifted his hand in triumph as he took the chequered flag a car's length ahead of Rosberg, with Cheever only half a second behind. 'It was the best race of my life,' said Ribeiro, and that went for the 100,000 spectators who had witnessed some superb driving on the toughest circuit in the world.

Alex Dias Ribeiro was born on 7 November 1948 in Belo Horizonte, Brazil. When Alex was eight, his father, who was a doctor, opened a practice in Brasilia, the new capital of Brazil. As the city was then in an early stage of construction, there were no schools, so Alex went to stay with his aunt in order to continue his education.

Alex had been brought up in a Christian atmosphere. From an early age his parents had taught him to believe in God, his grandparents had taught him to pray, and he continued to learn about religion from his aunt, who was a missionary. However, in his early years he found Church-going boring and he regarded God more with fear than love.

The turning point came when the eight-year-old boy attended a seven-day mission in the small country town where he was living with his aunt. One night, the preacher asked the congregation if anyone wished to accept the Lord. Not fully understanding what he was doing, Alex raised his hand. The following Sunday, Alex was the youngest of those who gathered on the river bank for baptism. He recalls how he felt as he emerged from the water. 'There was no doubt about it, I felt a completely new person. I noticed several changes in my life straight away. For instance, I had felt very unhappy and resentful at having to live away from home—now I accepted it and began to enjoy life again. I have always liked to make things. At that time I was building model aeroplanes, but I just hadn't enough patience and sometimes I would just smash them on the floor in my rage. Now I found I had patience and a new peace of mind. My new-found faith also helped me to cope with changing schools seven times.'

At the age of eleven, Alex fell in love with motor racing. A saloon car race was held as part of the celebrations at the official Inauguration of the city of Brasilia in 1960. 'That's it', Alex said to himself, 'I'm going to be a racing driver.' From that moment, he began to prepare himself for the day when he would sit behind the wheel of a fast car.

He could already drive, having learnt by watching his father and then practising on the side roads. But for the time being, the only racing he did was with model slot-cars or on his skateboard and bicycle. His father gave him a motorcycle when he was fourteen, and besides tearing around on it, he spent hours taking it to pieces and re-assembling it, learning valuable lessons in practical engineering. He also began working on a friend's Go-kart*.

Alex knew that, at eighteen, he would have a driving licence but no car. In his prayers he asked that God would give him a car; he even specified the model—a Renault Alpine GT. He got a car, although not in a way he could have foreseen. A week before Alex's eighteenth birthday, his father had a serious road accident, which put him in hospital for six months. His car, a Volkswagen Beetle, was a write-off, and he gave the remains to his son. Working long hours at weekends, Alex and three teenage friends built from the wreckage a 'Clubman' type sports car. They entered it for a six-hour race at Brasilia. Drawn at the very back of the starting grid and up against some very expensive, purpose-built cars among the thirty-three contestants, Alex and his co-driver achieved the seemingly impossible, finishing second behind an Alfa GTS.

Alex felt that God was opening the way for him to take up racing and was also giving him an opportunity to witness to Christ. From a magazine he cut the slogan *Jesus Saves*

*Mini 'car' driven by motor cycle engine.

and stuck it on the windscreen of the car, although, as he admits, 'At the time my ego was big and my Jesus not so big in my life'.

Because their car was the first built in Brasilia, Alex and his friends received much publicity and, as a result, their workshop became very popular. They decided to form their own business, which they called Camber Cars. It was hard work for eighteen-year-old Alex and his three younger friends. The two who had left school worked during the day; Alex and the other boy worked from 6 pm to 10pm at night, servicing and repairing their customers' cars. During the day, Alex was preparing to enter University, and in 1968 he began studying Engineering at the University of Brasilia. However, he was disappointed by the theoretical nature of the course, and in his second year he changed to a Business Management and Publicity course, which was much more relevant to his immediate interests.

During this time, the four friends continued to race their car, known as the Camber PT1, but apart from a few second places, the results did not do justice to the hours and money spent on it. Unable to devote sufficient time to a degree course in addition to the business and racing, Alex withdrew from University in his third year. It was decided to give up racing the Camber PT1 and concentrate on building up the now flourishing garage. Alex found he could not give up motor racing altogether and took up Go-karting again, a much less expensive form of racing, and quickly earned a reputation for himself, winning the Brazilian Championship in 1970 and 1971.

Those years were important to Alex's growth as a Christian. 'I joined a group who met for prayer and praise; through them I had an experience of the Holy Spirit, which changed me inside. I was twenty-one at the time and, until then, motor racing came before everything else. Now some words of Christ took precedence in my life: "But seek ye first the Kingdom of God, and His righteouness; and all these things shall be added unto you." (Matt. 6 v.33) Goals I had previously failed to reach, I now found I could attain—with God's help. Racing was still very important to me, but now I was increasingly concerned to use it as a means of getting the Christian message across.'

In 1971, Formula Ford* racing came to Brazil. With the help of his father and three businessmen, a Formula Ford car was purchased and a racing company established called 'Power'. Alex found several sponsors and, by the end of the year, was able to buy the car outright. His racing in this first season was not a success. He was trying too hard to win and, consequently, drove recklessly and was involved in a number of accidents, fortunately sustaining nothing worse than a broken wrist and injured pride.

At that time, the best racing team in Brazil was that sponsored by Hollywood, the country's largest manufacturer of cigarettes. Their team manager was impressed with Alex's determination and invited him to drive for them. Alex now faced a dilemma. He knew that there were some Christians who were strongly opposed to smoking. 'I put the problem to the Lord and prayed hard about it. I had another two invitations, but then those two doors closed and I was left with Hollywood; I accepted their offer.' His first race for Hollywood was in Brazilia, where he won, driving a Porsche 910 sports car. He now became successful in Formula Ford and was the runner-up in the 1972 Championship of Brazil.

Meanwhile, Camber Cars had continued to expand and now employed ten mechancis. Alex decided to concentrate on racing and sold his interest in the company. He moved to Sao Paulo, where he became Hollywood's Formula Ford supervisor, driving and directing the preparation of the cars. It was a very successful year. Alex took the chequered flag in seven Formula Ford races, winning the Brazilian 1973 Championship, and was ranked the top driver racing in Brazil itself.

'It was a very good year in *all* respects. When I moved

*Single-seater using standard Ford engine.

to Sao Paulo, the Lord put me in touch with other Christians, who supported me wherever I was driving. They put up *Jesus Saves* banners around the track and distributed a leaflet I had written entitled *Grand Prix of Life*. I'll never forget what happened after I had won the first race of the Championship. Some of my supporters had brought guitars, and as I stood on the winner's rostrum, they began to sing the chorus 'Jesus Saves'. The usually noisy crowd went absolutely silent for three minutes while the group sang, and then burst into loud applause. This became a regular feature whenever I won, and attracted considerable publicity in the Press and on TV.'

After becoming Formula Ford Champion, Brazil's largest circulation newspaper featured Alex in an interview headlined *Jesus Saves*. 'It gave me an opportunity to explain that the slogan referred to God's love in Christ, who died on the cross for man's salvation, and did *not* mean that God would save me from the dangers of motor racing! I felt as though I had been able to preach a mini-sermon to the paper's 450,000 readers, and this further convinced me of the potential for Christian outreach that motor racing gave me.'

In 1973, Alex paid his first visit to England, taking part in a couple of races to gain experience in Formula 3* racing. He crashed at Thruxton and came eighth at Brands Hatch. The following year, he moved his base to Wymondham, Norfolk, to compete for the British Formula 3 Championship. Sponsored by Hollywood, and driving a GRD 374, Formula 3 car, he took three first places and seven second places, and became runner-up to Brian Henton, winner of that season's championship.

Motor racing is a dangerous sport and Alex has had a number of accidents. Probably the worst was at the Snetterton track in Norfolk, where he was testing the new

*International formula using 2–litre production based engine with restricted power output.

GRD 374, Formula 3 car. After four warming-up laps he approached the notorious Russel bend at full throttle. It was a blind S, the scene of many crashes, including a fatal accident only a few weeks before. As Alex threw the car into the first leg of the S, the car spun and he found himself hurtling backwards. The car hit the bank at over 120 m.p.h. and it was thrown high into the air. 'Suddenly I found myself head down some fifteen feet above the ground. Everything seemed to happen in slow motion. I let go the steering wheel and tucked my arms between my legs in the hope that they would not be broken. Only God could help me now; all I could do was to pray for a soft landing.' The car nose-dived, cartwheeled and rolled over six times. It lost all four wheels and the bodywork, radiator and aerofoil wing flew off in all directions. What was left of the car came to rest on its side. For a moment Alex thought that the warm oil that covered his face was blood. Gingerly he unfastened his safety harness and crawled from the wreckage of the cockpit. It had happened right in front of his mechanics who now stood paralysed with shock. He walked slowly towards them. Then they ran forward and hugged him, hardly able to believe that he had survived without a scratch. The car was a total wreck. Alex took a philosophical view of the incident. 'I believe the safest place to be is at the centre of the Lord's will. If He wants to keep us alive, all right. If the worse comes to the worst, it's just the beginning of eternal life.'

The manufacturers of the March car saw Alex's potential and invited him to partner Gunnar Nielson, driving for their Formula 3 work's team in the 1975 season. The same year, Alex married his wife Barbara and moved to Bicester, where the March cars are built. At the end of the year, Alex was runner-up in the BP Formula 3 European and British Formula 3 Championships. Unfortunately, the season was marred by his involvement in a series of crashes and he gained a bad reputation, so much so that he tended to get the blame, whether he was at fault or not. The most publicised crash was at Monaco, an important race for up-

and-coming drivers as the winner could expect to be considered for a place in a Formula 1* team. With five laps left, Alex was driving comfortably in the lead, when looking in his mirror he saw Tony Brise who, having driven through the pack, was now on his tail. It was a fight to the finish, for both were determined to win. Overtaking is notoriously difficult, as the race is run along the harbour and around Monaco's narrow, twisting roads. The competition was so fierce that several times their wheels banged. Then it happened. Alex, still in the lead, braked hard and Tony ran on top of his rival's car. Both cars were out of the race, although, miraculously, neither driver was injured. However, it was Alex who was blamed in the Press reports.

In 1976, Alex moved up to Formula 2. It was a year when the French Renault-Elf teams dominated the Formula, taking the first four places in the European Championship. Alex, driving a British March car, did well to take fifth place. At the end of the season he was very highly rated as a driver, and it was natural that in 1977 March 'promoted' him to partner Ian Scheckter in their Formula 1 team.

To drive in the World Championship Grands Prix is the dream of every racing driver. But for Alex, 1977 was a disaster. His best results were his eighth places in the German and Canadian Grands Prix; he also managed eleventh, twelfth and fifteenth placings, but was forced to retire in four races and failed to qualify in the remainder. His unsuccessful season with March reflected drawbacks in the design and development of the car, rather than any deficiency in his own ability. But, nonetheless, by the end of the season, Alex felt totally demoralised; his reputation as a driver was shattered, his career in ruins. He prayed that he might learn something from this painful experience. 'I came to see that when the Lord doesn't work *through* us,

*World Championship Grand Prix formula using 3–litre unsupercharged or 1½—litre supercharged engines.

He works *in* us; that this setback was necessary to prepare me for something he had in mind for me.'

At this point, it was suggested to Alex that he should form a *Christian* racing team, running a Formula 2 car without any advertising except the *Jesus Saves* decal. To turn the dream into reality would cost at least £100,000 in the first year. It seemed impossible. Alex returned to Brazil with little expectation. But on arrival, his former sponsor, Hollywood, offered him £25,000 to wear their name on his overalls. It was a fifth of the budget he would need to race in Formula 2 in 1978. Apart from Emerson Fittipaldi, Alex was now Brazil's best known driver and so, with renewed hope, he began to approach companies for sponsorship. But, at the end of four depressing months, after contacting thirty companies, he had not a penny more.

With the new season about to start, Alex decided that he had no alternative but to quit motor racing. Sadly, he went back to his original sponsors to return the money. They asked, 'How many races could you do with our money?' Alex replied that it was enough to buy one car, one engine, and compete in three races. They said, 'Go ahead and do the three races'. They also told him that he need not put their name on the car itself. This meant that the car now 'advertised' *Jesus Saves* exclusively.

So, at the start of the 1978 season, *Jesus Saves Racing* came into being. Alex recruited three mechanics, one of whom, Alastair MacQueen, was a Christian. But, with two races gone and no prize money from either, the situation was critical. The next race was at the Nurburgring, probably the most testing circuit a driver can face. 'Alastair and I talked it over and felt that it would be right to pray that we might win the race and so have the money to carry on. So we claimed the victory in the name of the Lord and prayed like mad. And the Lord gave us the victory in the most amazing way—we won by one tenth of a second!' The motoring Press took the point, the headlines said it all: 'Jesus really saves', 'Alex resurrected', 'Jesus on top, Alex at the wheel', 'Alex in a state of grace', 'Ribeiro flies at the

Ring protected by a very unusual Sponsor'. That one victory gave more publicity to the *'Jesus Saves'* message than all the previous races put together. To Alex it was 'a response to prayer and confirmation that the work we were doing was the will of the Lord'.

With the prize money they could now take part in the next race. Furthermore, the manufacturer's of the car's engine were so impressed by the Nurburgring success that they lent the team another engine and offered to be responsible for the expensive rebuilds which are necessary after each race. With renewed enthusiasm the team travelled to Pau in France. But in the race itself Alex had a couple of minor accidents, twice losing the nose of his car, and consequently could finish only tenth. However, with some prize money and the start money they were able to go on to the next race at Mugello in Italy. A brand new engine was installed but to their dismay it blew up during practice. Hastily, they replaced it with the rebuilt spare engine and Alex came eighth. This was disappointing but at least he had finished and was able to collect the start money—it was just enough to take them on to Vallelunga, near Rome. During the first practice, Alex crashed and although he was not hurt the car was badly damaged. Using all their remaining spare parts, the mechanics rebuilt it in time for the next practice. In the race itself, Alex was lying fifth when the engine began to misfire; he struggled on, but with only twelve laps to go he was forced to retire. It was yet another serious setback.

Back in England Alex received £2,000 from an unexpected source, and this enabled him to go to France for the next race which was at Rouen. Alex was the fourth fastest qualifier and was lying fourth in the race itself when a tyre began to leak air. He stopped to change the wheel and could finish only twelfth. At Donnington, England, although he was second fastest qualifier, in the race he was left on the starting grid with an overheated clutch. In trying to make up lost ground, he hit another car and was out of the race. At Nogaro, France, he retired halfway through the race;

he was seventh at Enna, Sicily, and ninth at Misano, Italy. There was now no money left to enable the team to compete in the last race at Hockenheim in Germany. Alex hired his car out for the race and, although disappointed at not driving, he had the satisfaction of seeing the *Jesus Saves* message carried on the car before the thousands of spectators.

Altogether, the team had competed in fourteen races. It had taken strong faith to start with nothing and to tackle a racing season requiring a £100,000 budget. Nonetheless, the disappointing results after the success at the Nurburgring left Alex feeling very frustrated. 'It seemed as though every decision I had made in each race had been the wrong one. I even felt sad with the Lord for letting us down. There was one day when I had almost decided to give up being a believer, when suddenly the 'phone rang and I heard that we had a baby daughter. Somehow that changed everything, and I felt ashamed of my bad feelings and wept bitterly at my own lack of faith.'

Back in Brazil Alex worked hard to raise sponsorship for another season in Formula 2. He was promised £75,000, but half an hour before flying back to England he received a 'phone call to say that his main sponsor had withdrawn. Alex cancelled the flight. Then he had an idea. His younger brother, Fernando, also an enthusiastic Christian, was fast achieving success as a racing driver. Like Alex, he had graduated to Formula Ford after becoming Brazilian Go-kart champion. Alex approached his one other sponsor and asked if he could retain the money they had already given and race Fernando in European Formula Ford. It was agreed. With Alex as team manager, his sister Marta as secretary, Alastair MacQueen as chief mechanic and Fernando as driver, *Jesus Saves Racing* was now a fully Christian team. A brand new 1600cc Van Dieman RF 79 was bought with money from the sale of Alex's Formula 2 car and Fernando's old Formula Ford. With the limited sponsorship from a Brazilian cosmetics firm they began the season with little cash but high hopes.

Fernando was an instant success, not only winning races but establishing lap records, and becoming especially popular at Silverstone, his home track. By the end of the season he had won nine heats and three main races. In spite of starting the season a month late and then being out of racing for four weeks following a bad crash in which he broke his wrist, Fernando was runner-up in the RAC Formula Ford Championship; he was also fifth in the European championship—although he had only completed in half the total number of races. His slim, bright red car carried the text *Jesus Saves* in large white letters. He became a familiar sight on the winner's rostrum with the laurel wreath round his neck and holding a banner above his head emblazoned with the words, *Jesus is Lord*.

By now, Alex had his own workshop at the Silverstone Circuit, and during the summer of 1979, he moved house to Northampton. In May he was invited to drive in a Formula 2 race in Japan, and in September he was back in a Formula 1 car for the first time in two years. Teaming up with his fellow countryman, Emerson Fittipaldi, he drove for the Formula 1 Copersucar team at Imola in Italy. Although his drive came to an end when the car stuck in third gear after covering twenty-seven laps, it was an impressive comeback. As a consequence, Alex was invited to drive for Copersucar in America and Canada in the last two Grands Prix of the season and he was given a new car. Unfortunately, this turned out to be a personal disaster, for with it he failed to qualify in either race. This dashed his hopes for a place in a Formula 1 team in the 1980 season and Alex had to resign himself to the fact that his career as a Grand Prix driver seemed to be over.

The next logical step would have been for Fernando to drive a Formula 3 car for the 1980 season. Disappointingly, the *Jesus Saves* team was unable to obtain the necessary sponsorship. But because Fernando had achieved such success in his first season in England, he was in demand as a driver for one of the works team Formula Ford cars. After some negotiation it was arranged that he should drive for the manufacturer's of the Royale car, who also agreed that it should be painted red and carry the *Jesus Saves* decal. So the two-word 'sermon' continued to be preached to the thousands who watch motor racing.

Before the new season commenced, Alex returned to Brazil with his wife Barbara, and their young daughter Caroline. His ambition was still to run a *Jesus Saves* Formula 3 or Formula 2 team but this depended on being able to find adequate sponsorship. Meanwhile, back in England, Fernando had made a very promising start to the season. Then came a double disappointment for the two brothers. Ill health forced Fernando to retire from motor racing and he, too, returned to Brazil. Meanwhile Alex, unable to find sufficient sponsors, had to give up the idea of forming a new team. Although deeply disappointed, Alex accepted the situation and sought to discover what God was teaching him through the frustration of his hopes. At the time he wrote, 'It looks like the final defeat of Alex but the Lord will be victorious in this matter as He always is. What will happen tomorrow I don't know and I am not worried about that. From now on, not I, but Christ lives in me. My will is to be His will. The consequences of that only He knows.'

Alex now devoted himself to finishing an autobiography for the Brazilian market entitled *More Than Conqueror*. He published and promoted it himself and it has had a wide circulation. The publication of the book has led to many invitations to speak on his experiences as a Christian in motor racing. 'In fact,' he says, 'I have been able to reach more people for Christ through the book than I ever did when I was actually driving. So the Lord closed one door but, as He always does, He has opened another.'

7: Walking With Jesus

Brian Adams: Olympic Walker

Born 13 March 1949

The British team marched briskly down the ramp and through the tunnel into the vast Olympic stadium. They were greeted by a burst of cheering and clapping; everywhere flags were waving. Halfway down the home straight they saluted the Queen with an 'eyes right'. Brian felt a thrill of pride. He had represented his country many times before, but somehow this was different; this was *the Olympic Games*. His mind went back to the day when his career as a road walker began almost by accident.

At Roundhill Secondary Modern School, Leicester, the day commenced with morning assembly. That particular morning a teacher asked if anyone was interested in forming a walking team. Brian was not specially attracted to the idea. He had done a certain amount of cross country running and high jumping, but did not regard himself as much of an athlete. But a friend *was* interested and persuaded Brian to 'give it a try'. Somewhat reluctantly he learned the walker's technique of 'heel and toe', always keeping one foot in contact with the ground. The distances were not excessive—a mile or a mile and a half—but Brian trained hard, harder than some of the others to whom it seemed to come more easily. He became keen enough to join the Leicester Walking Club. This was fortunate because in 1965 he transferred with others of his age group to a new school where there was no walking team and his friends gave it up.

However, Brian continued to compete for his club and established himself as a member of their very successful

Junior Team. After a number of wins in local competitions, he was placed second in the Midland Youth Championships. He travelled with the club as widely as possible to gain experience and with the hope of bringing himself to the notice of the selectors of the national team.

In 1967 he was picked as third choice for the English team in a match against France, and because the first Junior International produced by the Leicester Walking Club. Although the French took the first three places in the 10,000m., Brian justified his selection by being the second British walker to finish. In the next couple of years he competed in four more Junior Internationals including a match against West Germany at the Crystal Palace, London, when he won the 10,000m. The year 1969 was a particularly good season for him when, in Britain, he won every race in which he competed, including the National 5 mile Junior championship.

Meanwhile, as Brian matured as an athlete, other important developments were taking place in his life. Brian's parents were not committed Christians but, nevertheless, at the age of ten he had started Sunday School of his own accord. He was confirmed in the Church of England when he was thirteen, sang in the choir and acted as a server at the altar. However, it did not mean very much to him and after a time he stopped going to Church altogether. One day in 1968, however, a friend invited him to her baptism which took place at a Baptist church in a nearby village. He was given a warm welcome at the door and everyone was so friendly that he decided to stay for the youth 'squash' after the service. He started going regularly to evening worship and the 'squash' which followed. He says, 'Gradually I came to realise that my life was incomplete and pointless if it was lived without God. He created me and gave me life, but I was leaving him out of it. The longing to be a committed Christian grew stronger and yet I did not do anything about it. Then, one summer evening a speaker at the Youth Squash challenged me to say 'yes' to Jesus. I took the step and committed my life to Christ.

Because it had all come about very gradually, I was not conscious of a dramatic change in my life. Nonetheless, I now had an assurance of being a Christian and, about six months later, in February 1969, I received believer's baptism.

Once a month the young people from Brian's church met with the young people of a neighbouring church. It was there that Brian met the girl who was to become his wife; her name was Joy. 'Even as a Christian of only a few months, I could see that God had got my life planned out. Both Joy and I felt sure that God had brought us together, a feeling that has been confirmed over and over again as the years have passed.'

In September 1970, Brian completed a five year apprenticeship as a technical engineer. He now felt that he wanted to put his athletic ability to better use. After attending a Technical College to gain some necessary qualifications, he commenced a three year Physical Education Course at Madeley College. It was also in 1970 that Brian began to compete as a Senior. During the next three years he gradually established himself as one of the top walkers in the club, and it was not long before he was leading the club home in most of the national events at 10 miles, 20km and 20 miles.

Brian was married in March 1973 and the following year, at the end of his College course, he moved back to Leicester where he began his career as a teacher and Joy took up a post in the hospital where she had originally qualified as a radiographer. They began to look round for a church to attend. One Sunday afternoon they were invited to a christening service at the Church of the Martyrs in the centre of Leicester. They liked the way the christening had been conducted and stayed for the evening service; afterwards they went back to the vicarage for the young people's meeting. They continued attending and before long they were made leaders of the youth group, opening their home each Sunday night to a growing group of teenagers. They both became members of the Parochial Church Council, and later Brian was made a churchwarden.

In 1974 Brian was eighth in the 10 mile National Championship and, in consequence, was selected to represent Britain in a match in Barcelona. It was not a full International but Brian won his race and later that year he was given his first full Senior International vest, competing against Poland in Warsaw.

The following year was the breakthrough in Brian's athletic career. Together with Roger Mills and Olly Flynn, he established himself as one of the top three walkers in the country. Early in the season he won the National 10km. championship, the first in a record achievement of five consecutive annual wins. He was selected for the 20km. race in a match against West Germany and Mexico and finished third, one place behind the reigning Olympic 50km. champion, the German, Kannenburg. Brian also managed to break the 'magic' 90 minutes for 20km. The Lugano Trophy World Team Championships were held later in the year. Brian finished second in the semi-final and sixth in the final of the 20km. He was the first Briton home, with a time of 87 minutes 46 seconds. This was his fastest time to date for the distance and had been bettered only by Paul Nihill, who had represented Britain three times in the Olympics.

1976 was the year of the Montreal Olympic Games. Although Brian was regarded by many as an automatic choice, he had to qualify by being one of the first three in a 20km. trial. As expected, Roger Mills, Olly Flynn and Brian went straight to the front of the trialists and remained there until the last three kilometres. It was at this stage that news reached them that the veteran Paul Nihill was closing fast on the leaders. Brian was in the vulnerable third place. With one kilometre to go, Paul passed him. Brian experienced a mixture of emotions—disappointment that he was out of the Olympic team and relief that he would not have to endure the pain and agony of another 20km. against world class competition. However, a race is never lost until the finish, and Brian steeled himself to keep going. Roger Mills was about thirty strides ahead, and Paul Nihill was steadily moving up to him. Suddenly, with 800 metres left, Roger collapsed and fell by the side of the road. Brian walked on with renewed energy and finished in the all-important third place.

Brian was in the Olympic team, after all. He was convinced that God was in control of this situation and that he was going to Montreal because God wanted him there. 'God had obviously got something he wanted to teach me. Meeting other Christian athletes, mainly from America, made me see that Jesus wanted to be Lord of my racing and that it was something he could use. There were particular opportunities as we mixed with men and women from the Eastern bloc countries. I met one competitor who passed on seventy Bibles to athletes who were unable to acquire one in their own country. One Lithuanian wept for joy when, for the first time, he saw a Bible written in his own language.'

Brian was determined to finish among the first ten in the Olympic 20km. walk. After completing the initial two laps of the track within the stadium, he glanced up at the giant score board to ensure that he was starting out at the correct pace. Then the competitors went up the ramp and out of the stadium and began the first of eight circuits of the Botanical Gardens. At this stage Brian was content to find himself in twentieth place, but gradually he worked his way nearer the front until by the 15km. mark he was ninth. However, the pace began to tell and he could not pull clear of two of the competitors who were challenging him. At the end of the eighth circuit he had slipped back into eleventh position. 'Coming down the slope into the stadium I overtook a Russian, but no sooner had I gone by him than an Italian passed me. I hung on to this position and was able to enjoy the excitement of completing the last lap, finishing in a time of 90 minutes 46 seconds. It was slower than I had hoped but I was the first Briton and first

Commonwealth walker home. It was an experience I will treasure all my life.'

Brian applies his Christian faith to racing as much as to any other aspect of life. He believes in the power of prayer but says, 'I don't ask God simply to give me victory or even to give me the strength and speed to enable me to be the first to break the tape. God has designed and built man with bones, muscles and nerves. It is up to *me* through hard work and concentrated training to develop stamina, strength and speed to the optimum. So what I pray is that my preparation and my tactics during a race may be right'.

Brian's next major target was the 1978 Commonwealth Games at which the road walk was over a distance of 30km. In preparation Brian spent most of the 1977 season building up stamina by competing at 50km. At this distance he was seventeenth in the World Team Championships, although, again, the first Briton to finish. The National 50km was a closely contested race. One of the competitors went off at an extremely fast pace, but Brian stayed with the chasing group, which proved to be a wise decision. In the closing stages it was a battle between himself and John Warhurst, the reigning Commonwealth champion. Eventually, Brian pulled away and won in a time of 4 hours 25 minutes.

Brian went to the Commonwealth Games at Edmonton, Alberta, confident of winning a medal and hopeful that it might be the Gold. The 30km. walk took place on a very hot day and many of the walkers were affected by the temperature. At the three-quarter mark, Brian had moved into the Bronze medal position, but gradually the heat sapped his stamina and it took all his reserves of strength to win the battle for fourth place. At first, Brian was bitterly disappointed at his performance. It was ironic that the race was won by his team-mate, Olly Flynn, whom he had beaten at the Olympic Games. But afterwards he tried to see his defeat from a Christian perspective. He remembered Paul's words to the Colossians (3.23): 'Whatever you are doing, put your whole heart into it, as if you were doing it for the Lord and not for men . . .' 'I reasoned', says Brian, 'that in God's eyes the first one across the line is not always the winner. He is concerned that we put everything into a competition, physically, emotionally and mentally, and that we don't give up when the going becomes hard. This means that we might be defeated by an opponent and yet still declared a winner by God. Realising this and knowing when I have given everything in a race has helped me to accept defeats and disappointments.'

In spite of his failure to win a medal at Edmonton, during the 1978 season Brian won a medal in all six of the National championships, including a victory in the National 10km. for the fourth consecutive year. He repeated his success at 10km. in 1979 but, because of an injury, his results for the remainder of the season were disappointing.

1980 was the year of the Moscow Olympics. But in December the previous year, Russia had invaded Afghanistan. As a result, Britain was divided on the question of whether to withdraw from the Games in protest. Individual athletes were faced with the agonising decision whether to make themselves available for selection if it was decided to send a team. As one of the country's top walkers, Brian stood a good chance of selection. In March, after much thought and prayer, he made the decision not to compete. Nonetheless, he decided to take part in the Olympic trials in order to prove to himself and to others that he was good enough to go, and was not simply opting out in case he did not get selected. In fact, in the first two trials he finished third.

Brian decided to withdraw. In a statement made to the Press he explained his reasons. 'I am a practising Christian and I cannot agree to compete in a country where my fellow Christians and dissidents in general are being unfairly treated. I came to my decision some time ago and recently informed the British Amateur Athletics Board of my feelings. I felt it only fair to let them know in good time—and the other walkers know of it, too. At the moment the big issue is Afghanistan, but while I do not agree with what the Russians have done there, my decision was made on purely religious grounds. I want no part of any regime which is responsible for putting Christian and other people in prison. There are also reports of many people being shipped out of Moscow for the duration of the Games rather than expose them to mixing with Western visitors. I really cannot lend myself to anything like that. I enjoy my sport but my religious beliefs come first. I feel the matter of competition is up to the individual and I have no quarrel with those athletes who decide to compete in Moscow. Although I'm not going, I shall be sending my best wishes to those who do.'

Without the pressures of preparing for the Olympics, Brian was able to ease up slightly on his training—the first time in ten years. He also found it possible to enjoy his racing more, and that summer secured third place in the National 50km. and fifth in an International 50km. in Paris. The following year, 1981, Brian was sixth in both the National 10 miles and 20km. At the time of the 20km. his club, the Leicester Walking Club, held all five National Championships, the first time this had been accomplished by any club. In August he was third in the 3,000m. at the AAA Championships, won by his old rival, Roger Mills, in a UK allcomers record.

In spite of training and racing, Brian makes time to play an active part in the life of his local church. When they moved to Sheffield in December 1978, Brian and Joy joined Greenhill Methodist Church. There they became co-leaders of the Senior Department of the Sunday School, and later, they started a mid-week 'Key Club' for the 11 to 13 year olds, which they held in their own home.

In 1981, Brian and Joy joined with a group of people from their neighbourhood to form the South Sheffield Evangelical Church. For two years they met in borrowed premises but, in December 1983, began building their own church and ancillary buildings. Much of the work has been done by the church members themselves. Apart from sharing in this voluntary labour and keeping up his training schedules, Brian has made time to lead the church '16 years plus' youth group. His minister says of him, 'He is a Christian who has a very firm commitment and gives a very clear witness, an unobtrusive person who is quiet, thoughtful and co-operative. He is someone whose Christian humility and graciousness has not been altered by success.'

Two important events the following year were the birth of a son, Nathan, in April and Brian's fourth position in the National 10 miles race. This earned him a place in the British team versus Spain. As it happened, this was to be Brian's last International and it was fitting that he was selected as Team Captain.

Without the spur of international competition, Brian felt he needed a new challenge. This presented itself mid-way through the 1983 season. He had already shared in his club's victories in the National 10 miles, 20km. and 35km. team events. He realised that if he could attempt the two remaining Nationals, the longer distances of 50km.(31 miles) and 100km.(62 miles), he stood a chance of being a member of the winning club team in all five Nationals in one season—a feat no one else had accomplished. Once again Brian scored points to help Leicester Walkers win the 50km.—the longest distance at which he had ever competed. It was with some misgivings that, two months later, he took part in the much longer 100km. To Brian's delight, his team not only won the event but he came in first! As a result, Leicester achieved the 'Grand Slam' for the second time and Brian became the first walker to win gold team medals for all five distances in the one season.

The following year through illness, Brian was unable to compete in the 35km., and due to the arrival of a second son, Simeon, was unable to start the 50km. However, at the end of July, Brian decided to tackle the gruelling two-day 100 miles walk. It was the first time he had competed at this distance, but after thirty miles, he went into a one mile lead which he maintained to win in a time of 17 hours 39 minutes. In September, Brian won the last London to

Brighton Road Walk. Due to the hazards caused by heavy traffic, this famous event has now been discontinued.

Brian has found that his ability as an athlete has given him many opportunities to speak about his Christian convictions. The night before flying out to the Montreal Olympic Games he had attended a 'Christians in Sport' dinner in London. He became involved with the newly formed organisation and, in consequence, received many invitations to speak at various Christian groups. He has also spoken at secular meetings and dinners, as well as in schools and sports clubs.

Brian's most public means of witness as a Christian is the personal slogan he uses, *Walk with Jesus*. He borrowed the idea from the American 800m runner, Madeline Manning-Jackson whom he met at Montreal. He noticed that whenever she was asked for her autograph, she always added the words, *Running for Jesus*. Brian, too, began to add his slogan, with its similar double meaning, when he gave his autograph. The slogan is useful as an immediate point of recognition as he discovered when he was at the 1978 European Championships in Prague. The Czechslovakian girl who was assigned to the British team as interpreter was collecting autographs on a poster. Brian signed and wrote his slogan underneath. Seeing it, the girl smiled and whispered, 'So you are a Christian, too' and drew out a chain which she wore round her neck and showed him the miniature fish attached to it—a traditional Christian symbol. Brian felt thrilled that he had been able to establish contact with another Christian even in a Communist governed country.

When, later, Brian met the Brazilian racing driver, Alex Ribeiro, and saw the *Jesus Saves* decal on his car, he realised the value of displaying a Christian message publicly. As a result, Brian had his *Walk with Jesus* logo printed on his racing vest and sweatshirt, and on the sun-strip on the windscreen of his car.

In spite of having reached the age at which many athletes would have retired, Brian intends to carry on walking, although at a less competitive level. He says, 'I want to spend more time with my family. I also want to take up new opportunities for Christian work, for instance, the Y M C A has opened a new 'Fitness Clinic' which needs staffing and there is a 'Christians in Sport' support group which has just started in the area. In one way or another, there is still plenty of "Walking with Jesus" to do.'

8: Heading for Goal

Alan West: Professional Footballer

Born 18 December 1951

Alan had always loved ball games. As far back as he can remember he was perpetually kicking a ball about. His father was very keen for him to become a footballer and when he was four years old Alan was given his first football kit to wear. The first team he played for was that of the local Cubs. They had a good team and won a couple of trophies and the local cup. Alan was very fast and played outside right; he was noted for the way he would slip the ball past the full back and dash for the goal. He also played for the Leigh Street Junior School and later for the Greenfield Street Secondary Modern, both in his home town, Hyde. He changed his position to that of inside forward, and although only eleven, during his first year at Greenfield Street, he was picked to play in a team of fifteen year olds. The other players towered over him and in one game, as he went to head the ball, another player kicked at it and connected with Alan's head—he needed six stitches as a consequence. Alan played for each of the school's teams and was made captain of the Senior XI. In his third year he was picked for N.E. Cheshire, and in his fourth year he played for Cheshire Schoolboys.

When Alan was fourteen years old, something happened to exceed his wildest dreams. His school was playing a local school team and Alan had scored two or three goals. Mr McBride, one of the rival school's teachers, recognised his talent and said he would try to get him a trial with a professional club. So, during the next school holiday, Alan went for a week's trial with Burnley, then a top First

Division team. A few days later, Harry Potts, the Manager, contacted Alan's parents with an offer for Alan to sign Schoolboy forms with the promise of his becoming an apprentice professional when he left school. News travels fast in the Soccer world and within a couple of days Alan was also approached by Manchester United. He now had to make the difficult decision which club to join. He was tempted by the opportunity presented by Manchester who, with Bobby Charlton and Denis Law, were then at their peak of performance. However, he eventually decided to sign with Burnley where he felt he might have a better chance of making the grade and becoming a full-time professional footballer. Every school holiday he went to Burnley for a week to train with the Club and get to know the other players.

He left school at the earliest opportunity. Finishing on a Friday, he moved into digs in Burnley on the following Monday. He was only fifteen and felt like a little boy among men. The daily training routine was very strenuous but Alan matured fast, and during his first year with Burnley he played midfield for both the 'B' and 'A' teams. His biggest thrill that season was to play in the team that won the FA Youth Cup. The next year he progressed from the 'A' team to the Reserves and, at eighteen, his ambition was realised when he was picked for the first team. By his nineteenth year he was playing regularly for the Burnley First Team. To crown his success he gained a place in the England Under–23's, played against Wales, and was picked as a substitute for the games against Scotland and East Germany.

Then came a set-back. Alan lost his place in the First team. He had a dispute with the Club over a new contract and played the next two years in the Reserves. He was bitterly disappointed. At the end of his contract, Alan was transferred to Sunderland. The transfer lasted only three days. He failed a medical test on the results of a spinal X-ray and came back to Burnley. He now thought his career as a professional player was finished. But three weeks after his return to Burnley he was bought by Luton for £100,000. It was October 1973 and Alan was twenty-one. Managed by Harry Haslam, Second Division Luton were well set in the promotion race. Alan played well in the First team, and at the end of the season Luton gained promotion to the First Division.

The Club made a disastrous start to the 1974/75 season, and had gained only nine points by Christmas. Bottom of the League, they were virtually written off, but in the new year Alan was made captain and the team staged a revival. However, it came too late. At the end of the season Luton had climbed to third place from the bottom, but were still one point behind Spurs. This meant that they lost their place in the First Division. The next season they played well and only just missed promotion. That summer, from May until August, Alan went to America to play for the Minnesota Kicks; it was the first of several visits.

That trip was the turning point in Alan's life. He had married his wife Cathie two years before, and they now decided to travel to the United States via New Zealand, where her parents had gone to live. As their jet powered its way above the white, fleecy clouds, Alan allowed his mind to wander back across the past few years. In many respects life was good. He trained hard and played hard, but there was always time for the kind of social life he and Cathie enjoyed at the bars, night clubs and discos. Life indeed *seemed* full, satisfying and exciting.

Alan well remembers their arrival in New Zealand: 'As our plane taxied to a halt we saw Cathie's father and mother waving to us. We found, to our surprise, that some twenty of their friends had also come to greet us. That evening, they all joined us for a welcome party; we were overwhelmed by the unexpected warmth and friendship shown to us by people who were complete strangers. Equally surprising was the change in Cathie's parents. When we had last seen them they were on the brink of divorce—now they seemed to have fallen in love again; in fact, they were like two new people. In their letters they had told us that it was all a result of their Christian conversion. But as neither Cathie nor I were in any way religious, that meant nothing to us. We soon discovered that the other guests were Christians, too, and we could not help but notice that they seemed just as happy and content with life.

The next day was Sunday, and Cathie's Mother and Father asked us if we would like to go to their church. Normally we never went to church but decided we'd go just to please them. We were in for another surprise. There was such tremendous joy, life and sincerity in the worship—it was so different from what we had imagined. We were very perplexed and felt we needed to find out what made these folk so different.

During the week we talked to a lot of people and asked many questions about the Bible, God, and life in general. The following Sunday we went to church again, but although it was another lively service, we somehow felt like two people on the outside of a fence. Until now, our hopes for the future had all centred around football, getting a better home, a bigger car, and having a good time. Now we were beginning to feel that something *was* missing in our lives; we just weren't in on the love, joy and contentment these Christian people seemed to possess.

On the eve of my departure for the States, we were invited to the home of Rene, one of my in-laws' many new friends. It was a night we will never forget. We had only gone for ten minutes, but as it happened we stayed for nearly three hours. Rene spoke of the love of Jesus Christ which she had discovered for herself and which we could know because Christ had died for everyone, and His love was for us, too. I remember there was a bright orange rug in front of the open fire and I sat staring at it, lost in thought. Inside me a war was raging; we were being brought face to face with Christ, but I didn't feel ready to change my life. I knew we must get out before we were involved any deeper.

As I stood up, Rene asked if she could pray for us before we left. "Dear Lord," she prayed, "help Alan and Cathie

110

to know that you have died for their sins, and may they open their lives to your love." Suddenly, Cathie broke down and wept. Running across the room to Rene she knelt by her side and said, "Lord, come into my life, please, please . . ." Cathie's Mum came to me, the tears rolling down her cheeks. "What about you, Alan, what about you?" she cried. Something inside me seemed to give way and I heard myself reply, "When Cathie's finished, *I'm* ready." It was as though we had each been waiting for the other. I fell on my knees, I hadn't a clue what to say. Somehow the words came, "Lord, forgive me, forgive all my past and fill my life." It was as if a weight had been lifted from my shoulders. Joy welled up within. I was free! We were all laughing through our tears.

Straight away we went up to the pastor's home where a meeting was in progress. Grown men wept for joy when they heard what had happened. "We've been praying for this for that last two years," we were told, "now you must be baptised." "But I'm due to fly to the States tomorrow," I protested. "That's no problem," one of them replied, "I've a swimming pool in my garden, we can all meet there in the morning." So, in the grey light of dawn, Cathie and I were baptised in the icy water of a garden pool! An hour later I was at the Airport. As I was about to board the 'plane, someone pushed a Bible into my hands and said, "Read this, have faith, trust in God and He'll see you through."

And He has. From that moment our lives started to change. I stopped swearing—and that's not easy for a professional footballer, Cathie gave up smoking, we found we had no desire to go out drinking and 'living it up'. We were no longer concerned about material things because we had found a new source of satisfaction and contentment. Our marriage began to blossom afresh and our love to deepen. We learned how to pray and to find help in the Bible for our daily needs. Even my Soccer improved! I had much more will to win and work hard. On or off the field I knew I had to show an all-round Christian attitude because there were a lot a poeple watching me and just waiting for me to slip up.

I'd been very apprehensive about what the other Luton players might say when they found out that I had become a Christian, and I prayed that the Lord would show me how to tell them. About a month into the new season, several of us were in the big bath after a match, when one of the lads said to me, "There's something different about you, Alan, you have definietly changed, we've all noticed. What happened when you were away?" That gave me the opportunity to share with them how Christ had come into my life. At first some of the lads were a bit wary of me, expecting me to become some kind of holy Joe. But they soon got over that and since then they have always respected my convictions.'

The news of Alan's conversion reached the wider public early on in the season. Whilst travelling by coach to an away game some of the team began asking Alan questions. Two newspaper reporters sitting opposite overheard and asked if they could report the news. The story appeared in the *Luton News* and *Evening Post*. 'That', says Alan, 'is how the Lord told all Luton; and when the story was told in the *Sunday People*, that's when the whole country got to know!' As a result, Alan began to receive some good natured heckling from the spectators: 'Come on, Westy, get your Bible out,' and 'you've not being praying hard enough,' or 'Go on, Moses, lead the Lutonites to the Promised Land!' Later in the season, when the team was getting bad results and Alan was not playing very well, he had to suffer abuse of a more vindictive nature. As Captain, some of the supporters blamed him for the team's poor performance. It was a hard time, but Alan was encouraged by letters sent by many Christians who attended the games. It was a test of his faith but he matured as a Christian as a result.

In the 1975/76 season, Luton were sixth in the Second Division, just missing promotion, but in the following two seasons they were nearer the bottom of the League. When

David Pleat became manager in 1978, Alan was relieved of the captaincy. It was his new-found faith that helped him to overcome the initial disappointment.

Each summer Alan returned to the U.S.A. to play for the Minnesota Kicks, helping them to win the Western Division of the North American Soccer League (NASL) on four occasions. Arguably, Alan played his best football in America and was dubbed the 'Midfield Magician'. In a hypothetical NASL 'All-Star Team 1977' picked by a pool of players for *The Sporting News*, Alan was selected along with other famous players such as Gordon Banks, Franz Beckenbauer, George Best and Pelé. Alan was very popular with the large Minnesota crowd and in the '77 season was voted 'First team all-star', having a net club record assisting with eleven goals.

Kick, the official magazine of the NASL featured Alan in its edition of 29 April 1978: 'He's the "Magician", dancing, spinning down the sidelines, taking on an opponent, man-to-man, doing a quick side step or two and then he's gone, leaving that opponent in his wake as he dribbles along, kicking a pass to a team mate, setting up a goal or striding towards the sidelines to arch a perfectly-placed corner kick in front of the net.' Although the Minnesota Kicks would have liked him to extend his 'summer season' contract, the loan of players to other clubs has now been banned by the English Football Association.

Being a professional soccer player *and* a Christian has not been easy but it has given Alan the opportunity to talk about his Christian faith with people of all ages. Previously he had never spoken in public, but as a result of his conversion he found he was able to address a variety of audiences. He receives several letters a week requesting him to speak at youth clubs or to give his testimony at churches of all denominations. He coaches soccer at a number of schools and is in constant demand to take part in school assemblies. He enjoys addressing Men's Meetings and has also spoken at both Oxford and Cambridge Universities. He now limits his speaking engagements to one a week, and tries not to be away from home on Sundays so that he can worship at his own church.

Being prepared to 'nail one's colours to the mast' and speak in public about one's faith is a daunting responsibility as Alan has discovered. Mary Batchelor in *The Everyday Book* (Lion Publishing) tells how Alan was the guest speaker at a buffet supper held in Torquay. 'At the meal he chatted to the guest sitting next to him, who turned out to be a referee of league football, present because of his interest in sport. A few months later, when Alan's team was playing at Newport, he recognised the referee as his dinner companion at Torquay. The game began. About half way through, Alan tackled and the referee's whistle blew shrilly. He came running across to Alan, who had committed an unintentional foul. The referee asked his name in official tones, with no hint of recognition. Then, as he produced the yellow card, he challenged, 'What was all that about *Christians* in sport?' Alan could only reply that he had never claimed to be perfect. As a Christian, he is only too conscious of his failings and the forgiveness Christ gives. But he is very much aware that being a Christian in sport, as in every job, means that people are watching how he acts. The onlooker expects a high standard. What he does must back up what he says.'

Another consequence of becoming a Christian was the discovery Alan made that he could be used to win others to the Christian life. Alan frequently receives letters requesting advice and sometimes this leads to a personal encounter. For instance, when he had been a Christian for only four months, he was featured in the *Players Profile* in a match programme. During the interview for the Profile, he had been asked the question, 'What was the greatest moment in your life?' He had replied, 'Realising that God exists.' A week later he received a letter from Robin, a Luton fan who, because of a crippling disease, was confined to a wheelchair. It was a searching letter asking how anyone could believe in a God who allowed such suffering. Alan replied, explaining what had happened to his life. This was the start of regular correspondence and later Alan began to visit Robin and they became firm friends. Three years later, after going to church with Alan a few times, Robin became a Christian.

On another occasion, an eighteen-year-old girl turned up unexpectedly at Alan's home. It was a bitterly cold night and the girl was dressed only in a tee-shirt and jeans. She had run away from home and had many personal problems. Alan and Cathie took her in and the girl stayed with them for three weeks. She was impressed by the love and kindness they showed her and she began to ask questions. They told her how God had changed their lives and how He could help her, too. One morning they found her in tears. She confessed that her life was empty and that she needed something to fill it. She gave her life to Christ and from that day made a new beginning. She went back home and, after patching up the quarrel with her parents, she found somewhere to live, found a job and began attending church regularly. 'To-day,' says Alan, 'she is a completely transformed person.'

In the early 1980's Luton was still fighting for promotion to the First Division. Alan had to face keen competition for his place in the team. He has also had to fight a battle of conscience over the vexed question of Sunday football. In February 1981, as an experiment, a match was arranged for a Sunday morning between Luton and Orient. Normally, Alan and Cathie attended morning and evening worship at the Elim Pentecostal Church in Luton where they are members.

What should he do? Alan says, 'I gave this a lot of consideration. But football is my job, and many Christians have to work on Sundays. I'm not happy about agreeing to play, but as a 'pro' I feel I should play if I'm called upon. However, if football were to be played every Sunday, it might be a different matter and I would have to reconsider my position.' Ironically, in the end, Alan was not picked for the game.

In June 1981, for a fee of £45,000, Alan was transferred

to Millwall Football Club to help them with their drive for promotion. Alan said, 'I haven't found any real problems by joining a new club. I've been a Christian for five years now and feel fairly settled in my faith. It was much more difficult when I had to return to Luton after my conversion and prove I was a different person. Being a Christian does bring its own pressures, though. For instance, because I haven't been afraid to share my beliefs, people have sometimes been quick to criticise if they think I'm doing something wrong. There may well have been times when they were right. But I've never claimed I'm perfect, I've just said I'm a Christian.'

Alan's conduct on the field has been exemplary since he became a Christian. 'I like to think that being committed—whether it's to Jesus Christ, your family *or* to a football team—is part of your Christian life. I believe that God is interested in my job and in the way I play, in fact, I represent God when I'm out there playing. There's absolutely no doubt that I want to win as much as any member of the side and I give one hundred per cent, but if we lose it isn't the end of my world. There are often frustrations. For example, there may be times when you are 'dropped' from the team and you can't see why. It's in those difficult times that God becomes very real.'

At the end of the 1982–83 season, Alan left Millwall FC to take up a new challenge as player-manager of non-league Hitchin Town who were struggling to avoid relegation. Under his leadership the Club improved considerably and came sixth in the Isthmean Premier League. In the 1984–85 season, the side was handicapped by a series of injuries to key players. Alan brought in a number of younger players and the team retained a place in the League—to be renamed the Vauxhall-Opel League at the commencement of the 1985–86 season.

Apart from his career as Player-Manager, Alan has become Assistant Pastor at the Elim Church in Luton. He is also taking a correspondence course that could lead to him becoming a full-time pastor. For the time being, however, he will continue playing and await God's guidance for the future.

Alan realises that as a professional footballer he has a rare opportunity to witness to the Christian faith. 'When I'm out with the team I can show that I don't need six or seven pints of beer to bring a smile to my face. I also find that ordinary people can relate to me because I am a professional sportsman; for some reason people will listen, especially young people. I am also keen to reach out to other athletes and I am very much involved in the 'Christians in Sport' organisation as a member of the National Executive Committee, and I belong to the North London branch. At a recent CIS Sportsmen's Dinner there were 300 people there. I was able to invite the whole club along, with their wives and girl friends. About twenty-five came and there were others from Luton, Watford, Tottenham, Newport and other clubs as well as people from all kinds of sport. Cliff Richard came along and shared his faith and former professional footballers, Ritchie Powling and Derek Jefferson spoke about the change in their lives since they became Christians. I, too, welcome the opportunity to share my beliefs at these dinners and other meetings arranged by the organisation. I like to be positive. I tell people you don't become a Christian by being 'good enough'. It's all a matter of going to God to find that inner strength you need. You prove Christianity in that way in your own life.'

Family life is very important to Alan. He says, 'I wouldn't change the life I have now with Cathie and by boys, Benjamin and Josh. You look around and see marriages crumbling and people's lives in ruins. I can't describe what peace, joy and love in my life means to me. At the end of my working day I just love being at home—how many men can say that?'

Alan's witness to Christianity among professional footballers and others is quiet and sincere. He often waits until the other players ask him questions or open up a conversation on religion. He hopes that others hearing about his faith will find Jesus Christ for themselves. 'God filled a vacuum in my life,' he says. 'I want everyone to know that only the Lord can fully satisfy. Whilst I am a professional footballer I intend to take every opportunity I can to share the gospel. *That's my immediate goal in life.*'

9: Twin Talents

Jane and Jill Powell: All-Round Sportswomen

Born 19 January 1957

Identical twins, Jane and Jill, were taken to their first cricket match when they were only nine days old. As soon as they could walk they shared eagerly with their brother, Gary, in the family games of cricket—in the back garden of their Sheffield home or on the beach during the summer holidays. 'Everyone in Yorkshire plays cricket,' Jane says, 'and by the time we were five we were taking it quite seriously. As well as playing, we loved to watch matches, too, and one of us would always keep the score.'

The twins had a natural aptitude for sport and that particular co-ordination of hand and eye which is needed for success in any ball game. Their first achievement in team games came when they were eleven, and members of the Woodseats Junior School Rounders Team who, in 1968, were winners of the Junior Sheffield Championships. Later that year, the twins moved up to the Abbeydale Girls Grammar School*. There they played netball, badminton and hockey and took up cross-country running and athletics. By the time they were fourteen, they had both played for Sheffield Schools at hockey and badminton, and Jane had represented the city in cross-country running at county level. Jill showed exceptional promise at throwing

*Re-named Abbeydale Grange when it became a mixed comprehensive school. The school has produced five international sportspeople, including Sebastian Coe.

the javelin. She won the Yorkshire AAA Junior title and, three weeks later, the Junior Girls Javelin at the Yorkshire Schools Athletics Championships with a record throw of 30.72 metres.

Both girls excelled at badminton and at the age of fifteen claimed the honours at the 1973 Sheffield Schools tournament. They won the under–16 and under–19 doubles and then fought out a family battle in the under–16 and under–19 singles. Jane eventually beat her sister and went on to be part of a winning partnership in the under–16 and under–19 mixed doubles. Both girls were members of the Yorkshire team which won the under–16 National Schools Championships in 1973. The same year, Jill was one of the Abbeydale Grange team that reached the finals of the English Schools Netball Tournament and a member of the SW Yorkshire Junior team in the Inter-Counties Championship at the Crystal Palace.

The twins were still keen on cricket and welcomed the opportunity to play it more seriously. When they were fifteen, they happened to see an advertisement in a local newspaper in which the Sheffield Ladies Cricket Club was recruiting players. They applied and began playing for the Club. Although they were so young, Jane began to build up a reputation as a fast bowler and Jill as a batsman. The fact that they were identical twins caused considerable confusion, particularly when one person seemed to be fielding in two different positions! They added a new honour to their growing list of sporting achievements when they were both picked for the Yorkshire Junior team. Impressive performances in the National Six-a-side Women's Cricket tournament led to their selection for the England Junior (under–19) team. Jill also won national selection as an under–21 throwing the javelin for England in competition with Scotland and Wales.

Up to this point, the twins had been involved in practically every sport open to women. However, at a higher level of competition, they found it necessary to specialise. Jane concentrated on hockey and was selected for the North of England Junior XI, an outstanding team which won the Junior Regional Tournament. She was the first person from the Sheffield league to achieve this honour and was to play for the next three years, being appointed captain in her last year. The North side dominated Junior hockey during this period, winning the great majority of their matches.

Meanwhile, Jill, concentrating on netball, was in the Abbeydale Grange under–18 netball team which became NE England Schools champions for the second year running. She was also a member of the Sheffield under–21 team which went through the 1974 season undefeated. Having taken the Yorkshire and Humberside and North-East of England titles, the team's outstanding triumph was to beat the North-West to win the National Association of Youth Clubs' title. The following year, Jill was picked to play for England, the first south Yorkshire netball player to be selected at any level for the national side. She emerged from a gruelling two-day trial with 125 other contestants to win her place. The county team coach said, 'Jill never allowed herself to be put off by competition. Her ability to cope with the pressures of the trial singled her out. She is an outstanding player and a great sporting character.' Jill played at centre, a link position that exploited her pace and power. The team won against Wales and the Republic of Ireland but lost against Scotland.

Now eighteen, both girls were still as keen as ever on cricket. In the 1975 season, Jill was chosen to captain the East of England versus the West. Jane was also selected but was unable to play because of an injury received the previous week. Fielding at silly mid on, she had been hit by a fast moving ball and sustained two fractured ribs. She recovered in time to play in the England Women's Junior team against the Yorkshire Seniors; and Jill had the further honour of captaining the side. They went on to play a drawn game against the Young England (under 25), a match in which Jill scored 22 runs, and her sister 19.

Both girls are right-handed batsmen, Jane batting at number 5 and Jill at number 3. Jill bowls medium pace and Jane is a noted fielder. Jill says, 'Girls have to time the ball well when they're batting because they are not as strong as men.' Jane adds, 'It's quite true a lot of men come to scoff at women cricketers, but usually they end up applauding. Once the men actually see us they realise we can play the game and achieve a high standard of play.'

The twins left school in the summer of 1975. Up to that time they had always been together, sharing each other's lives and encouraging each other in the world of sport. Although they chose the same career in physical education, they decided it would help them as individuals if they enrolled at different colleges. So, in the autumn, Jill went up to Dartford College of Physical Education*, the country's top netball college, while Jane also went south, to Chelsea College of Physical Education†, at Eastbourne, a college that excelled at hockey. This was the twins' first experience of any prolonged separation. Jill felt very lonely; but worse than the unaccustomed loneliness was a general feeling of the emptiness of her life. She had always dreamed of success at sports but now, having already represented England at three sports, what next? Jill remembers how she felt at the time. 'When you've been chasing after success and suddenly you get there, you think, "Well, what *is* success, after all?" You then go on to the next thing you want to do and, as soon as you get there, you wonder, "Why did I want to get here, anyway? It is the same in sport as with material things, when you get everything that everyone else seems to want, you find there's nothing there, nothing concrete. There can be a feeling of pointlessness about life. I tried to fill the vacuum by living it up—parties, discos, drinking. . . . Then, one day, a friend happened to ask me, "Have you ever thought about this Jesus bloke? You should, you know, it's worth it."

'That phrase, "It's worth it" went round and round in

*now part of Thames Polytechnic.
† now part of Brighton Polytechnic.

my mind. I had many questions; for instance, who was this Jesus? Why should he make any difference to my life? I didn't understand my need of a new relationship with him. Although we had been brought up in a very loving family and went to Sunday School when we were young, Christianity didn't mean anything to Jane or me. Sunday School was just something else to do, like belonging to the Brownies. We had sat the Scripture examination for four years—in the fifth year we would have each received a Bible. However, when we were eleven we started training seriously for sports, and as that had to be on Sundays, we gave up Sunday School—so we never had our Bibles! Now, my friend suggested I should start looking in the Bible for some answers to my problems. I had to *borrow* a copy! When I began searching I was surprised to discover how relevant the Bible was to everyday life.'

'At the end of my first year at College I went home still with many questions unanswered. If I was going to follow this Jesus I wanted to know all the "whys and wherefores". I wasn't going to make a wild leap in the dark. It wasn't worth changing the whole of my life unless I went into it completely. Why did Jesus have to die? What difference would it make to my life if he really was alive today? As I read on, slowly it all began to fall into place and, gradually, I began to change. I can't look back and say that at a certain time on a particular day I was converted, but I do know that, by the end of August, it had happened. *I felt different inside*—I no longer felt that life was pointless; I began to see people in a different light.'

'When I went back to College to begin my second year, I found my attitude to sport had changed. Previously, I had been very temperamental and aggressive. I still had the will to win, but now instead of giving knock for knock, I had no impulse to retaliate. It didn't need a conscious effort to restrain myself. My overall attitude had also changed completely, particularly off the field, in my social life, for example. I never drank again, I never even thought about it; in fact, for months I didn't realise I had given it up.

There now seemed so much to see, so much to do, it was a totally new world that I was in. I can never understand why people say, "If I became a Christian I would have to give up so many things". Really you don't have to give up anything; you get so much more in return that it's a plus rather than a minus.'

'The other students noticed, of course. They said I had joined the "God squad" and become one of those "Jesus freaks". I didn't lose all my old friends, but I made a lot of new friends. Some of the other Christians kept to themselves in a "holy huddle". But because I was in the First teams, in fact, captain of two—a position highly esteemed in a PE college—I was able to bridge the gap between those who were Christians and those who tended to look down on them as rather spineless creatures. I joined the Christian Union, a meeting of students of all denominations. The first time I went, I had some way to walk and it was pouring with rain. I kept thinking, "whatever am I doing trudging through this rain to go to a meeting of Christians?" But I kept walking, and after that I attended regularly. For the first time in my life I went to church each Sunday and found this helped me to learn a lot more about being a Christian. Once a month several of us went to a local psychiatric hospital and visited the wards, singing to the patients. We also became active in the local community and local churches. We went about singing and speaking to different groups. My old friends said, "Jill has finally flipped it!"

'Becoming a Christian wasn't all plain sailing. In particular I made one big mistake. All my life I had wanted to be the best at everything I did and, at first, this was my attitude to Christianity—I wanted to be *the* best Christian. Yet the harder I tried, the more things seemed to go wrong. I became fed up with trying on my own to live a good life. I came to realise that I was not self-sufficient; everything I was had to come from Jesus rather than from me. In the end I suppose I made a general surrender to him, a complete giving in, which is hard on anybody's pride, especially mine. But it made all the difference; since then I have tried to rely entirely on Jesus.'

When Jill became a Christian, she wrote and told Jane of the 'new friend' she had found in Jesus Christ. 'I was very upset, at first,' Jane recalls, '*I* had always been my sister's best friend. I was the only one she had turned to, so why should she suddenly turn to someone else?'

Jane was curious to know what had affected Jill so deeply, so she borrowed a Bible to try and find out. 'I sat down,' she says, 'and opened the Bible at the first page and began to read—I remember I wasn't very impressed with the Book of Genesis!'

Jane talked to other students who were Christians to learn more about Christianity. She began attending meetings of the College Christian Union, slipping in quietly at the back, hoping she would not be too noticeable. She was noticed, however, and to her consternation, she heard that some of the girls were praying for her.

'Over the course of the next nine months,' she recalls, 'I came to realise that Jill hadn't gone stupid after all! Gradually things fell into place as I found what the Bible really had to say and saw the difference faith made to life. I concluded that Christianity was OK. And if it was alright for Jill, then it should be for me.'

'As with Jill, there was no sudden dramatic conversion, but bit by bit I gave my life to Christ. After one Christian Union meeting I went back with one of the girls to her flat. I said I knew I had to do something about becoming a Christian and we prayed together. Afterwards we walked along the Eastbourne seafront. It was a dark November night, but I saw the sky, the waves and everything in a way I'd never seen before. Soon after I wrote to Jill saying I had checked it out, and she'd be pleased to know that I'd become a Christian as well.'

When Jane began to attend Christian Union meetings openly and it became known that 'she had gone religious', it caused some surprise. 'It was then,' she says, 'that I realised that to be a Christian in today's society calls for a different kind of strength to that required in sport. I also began going to Sunday worship and was drawn into the family of the Central Methodist Church, Eastbourne, where the minister, the Revd David Dunn Wilson, greatly helped my growth in the Faith.' Later, she was received as a church member.

A number of other students used to attend the same church, and together they helped to rejuvenate the Young People's Group. There were several groups that needed the assistance of young people and Jane was amongst the first to volunteer to help run the '31 Club', a club for the deprived children of the neighbourhood, aged 3–15 years. Although the work was difficult and often frustrating, the numbers increased and the club was a success; Jane remained one of its most regular and long-serving helpers. Apart from the '31 Club', she also helped to initiate a 'Faith Tea' for a mixed age range. It was held at the church each Sunday afternoon at 4pm. Those who came brought their own food and took it in turns to lead the singing and prayers until it was time for evening worship. She also began what has become an annual fortnight's attendance at a CYFA summer camp.

Becoming Christians did not diminish the enthusiasm for sport of either of the twins. While at Dartford, Jill played for the PE college at netball, cricket and basketball. At the beginning of her second year, she went on a basketball tour of the USA, and in her third year was captain of the netball and cricket teams. She also played lacrosse, hockey and tennis. During her first year, she did not play in any county or national trials as she wished to concentrate on college sport. However, in her second year, she had county and national trials at cricket and was selected to play for Kent and for Young England against Junior England. She was also nominated as travelling reserve for the senior England team.

Meanwhile, Jane was playing hockey for Chelsea College and for Sussex. In her second year, the college won the British South-East regional tournament and topped the table in the Inter Physical Education Colleges Tournament. The following year, Jane captained the hockey team that retained the British Women's PE Colleges championship won the previous year. Chelsea won all five matches and Jane, with seven goals, was the leading scorer. In January, 1978, she was selected for the South of England in matches against the North and East, South Wales and the Midlands. She was even more thrilled to be chosen in March for the England 'B' team who won their matches against Wales, Ireland and Scotland.

While Jill played cricket for Kent, Jane was playing for Sussex. She also played for the South of England against Australia, and like Jill, played for Young England. In July 1977, both twins were picked for a trial for the England Women's cricket team, and this time it was for the *senior* national side. It was with great excitement that, later that month, they received a letter from Rosemary Goodchild, the Chairman of the England Women's Cricket Association, which read:

'Dear Jane and Jill,

I am writing on behalf of the WCA to inform you that you have been selected as Reserves for the England Touring Team in India, for the 2nd World Cup Competition in Dec. 1977/Jan. 1978.

This selection means you must hold yourself in readiness in case you are needed to travel with the party. . . .'

In mid-December, a weekend 'phone call changed Jill's plans for a Christmas holiday at home. The England selectors informed her that a tour member had dropped out at the last moment. Could Jill, as first reserve, make it? At first she could not believe her good fortune, and then it was a hectic rush to get ready for the flight to India. On Christmas Day she was in Calcutta. Although she celebrated her twenty-first birthday in Bangalore, she was still the youngest member of the tour by eight years. It was an exciting series with matches against India, New Zealand, Jamaica, Trinidad and Holland. England played well and won their way through to the Final in which they were narrowly beaten by Australia. When the English cricket season began, Jill was appointed captain of Young England against Holland, a game that the home team were on the way to winning when rain delayed play and the result was a draw.

Jill's attitude to winning and losing was very different from what it had been before she became a Christian. 'That completely changed my approach to playing cricket,' she says. 'Now it's no longer a case of winning at all costs but of trying to make the game entertaining to watch. I also take losing better. Instead of saying it was just bad luck or that the other team cheated, I am now able to admit when we lose because the other team played better. I try now to do well whether we win or lose.'

After leaving college in the summer of 1978, Jill started work as assistant to the Manager of Recreation at the Hemel Hempstead Sports Centre. Jane stayed on for a fourth year at Chelsea College. She continued to play hockey for her college and also played for the England Under–23 team, competing against Wales, Scotland and Ireland for the Canada Cup. England won all three games and Jane was described in the Press as the 'outstanding player of the tournament'. In the summer of 1979, Jill was playing county cricket for East Anglia, for whom she scored a career best of 127. The twins were both picked for the Young England match against the West Indies at the Oval, Jill acting as captain in a one day match which was lost by just 27 runs. Jill was also selected for the full England side against the West Indies. She was twelfth man in the first two Tests and two one-day matches, and played in the third Test and last one-day match. At twenty-two she was the youngest member of the team. Later, in a three day match at Canterbury, she was vice-captain of England v. The Rest.

At the end of her college course, Jane was unable to find a suitable job in the south, so she returned home and applied for the post as PE teacher at the City School in Sheffield. The first week she was there she came across some members of her young hockey team arguing about religion. She told them she was a Christian and shared her faith with them. One of the girls confided that she and her friend had been praying for three years for someone like Jane to come to the school. Together they started a school Christian Fellowship which attracted thirty to forty pupils at their weekly lunchtime meetings. Jane joined the Emmanuel Church in Waterthorpe, an ecumenical church on a new housing estate. She once more represented Yorkshire at hockey and cricket. She was also picked again as a left inside forward for the England Under–23 Hockey team who won the Canada Cup for the second consecutive year.

Jane's faith has had its effect on her approach to sport. 'Sport is often a win-at-all-costs thing. I used to be like that', she says. 'But God is not interested in us winning. He is interested in the way we take part.' For this reason, when playing hockey, she refuses to foul an opponent. She also believes that self-control is something important, especially for Christian sportspeople, as she explained to Malcolm Doney of *Today*. 'The number of times I've been taken out of a game—whacked across the knees—is incredible. Opponents can't believe it when I just get up. So far, with God's help, I've been able to control myself. The sports world is a difficult one. People think that because you're a Christian, you are weak. But it's the opposite. You've got to put up with people saying that, as well as the pressures of the sport itself.'

In January 1980, Jill started a new job as Recreation Officer of the London Borough of Hillingdon based at the South Ruislip Leisure Centre. When the cricket season began, the twins both played for Young England, Jill as captain. In May they took part in the trials for the England team to tour India at the beginning of 1981. To their delight, they were *both* selected and Jill was nominated as captain.

On January 10, the team flew out to Delhi. It was the first time the Young England side had toured and there followed a hectic seven and a half weeks. In travelling from match to match they covered over 25,000 miles mostly by coach or train, playing eleven matches in 48 days, and having only a day and a half free time! They played four one-day matches against the Indian XI, a couple of two-day matches against the South and North Zones, a one-day charity match, and five of the six scheduled Test Matches. The three-day Test series was played against the full India team, most of whom were very much more experienced in Test matches than the English girls.

England won the one-day International series by three games to one. Disappointingly, each of the Test matches ended in a draw. 'It was extremely frustrating,' said Jill. 'We kept losing the toss and the Indian team adopted a negative approach by batting slowly from the start. Their captain made the most difficult declarations, as in the last game when we were left with only thirty-five minutes to score 171!'

The English team were amazed at the popular support for women's cricket in India. Although the matches were televised, crowds totalled from 9,000 at Delhi for the first Test to 45,000 for the one-day International at Patna. But in the fifth Test, Jill was faced with an unexpected crisis when a riot erupted among the 35,000 crowd at Jammu. The circumstances in which it happened were unusual: when the girls reached the Maulara Azad Stadium at 8.45am, they found that it had been used previously for a military tattoo! The ground was damp and there were potholes, ruts and tank tracks all over the outfield. The England team protested that the surface was too dangerous to play on. While the crowd grew increasingly restless, the organisers had the pitch sprinkled with sawdust and the roller was brought on in an attempt to level the area. At 11am the umpires declared the field fit for play. Jill and her vice-captain consulted with the team and they took a unanimous decision not to play and informed their manager, Anne Sanders. Jill and Anne were called out to the centre of the pitch to face the Indian officials. The crowd were growing angrier and noisier. Jill prayed hard for courage as she was pushed and jostled by the organisers.

She repeated their refusal to play because of the dangerous condition of the ground.

When the crowd realised that the game was to be abandoned, they began to throw bottles and chairs on to the pitch. About 3,000 spectators marched from the east end of the ground to the north pavilion where the England team had locked themselves in their changing room. A brick was thrown through the window. The police struggled to hold back the spectators as they shouted abuse at the England team. Thoroughly frustrated, the angry crowd broke down some hoardings and set fire to them, while others, from a distance, pelted the police with stones, injuring several of them. The girls piled their kit bags against the door and, keeping very quiet, waited hopefully for their release. At last, after five hours, the police were able to smuggle them out of the ground in their riot vans. Jill comments, 'It was very frightening at the time, but it is nice that they were so keen to see us. It beats playing at The Oval with *no one* there!'

On the whole, however, it was an enjoyable tour. The women cricketers were treated like superstars. One morning they breakfasted with the Indian prime-minister, Mrs Gandhi, at her house in Delhi. The England 'skipper' was held in high esteem and was on show twenty-four hours a day. Every day Jill was interviewed on television and radio. The Indians were also fascinated to see identical twins and were continually taking photographs of them. Everywhere they went the cricketers were greeted by crowds, and it was particularly encouraging for Jill and Jane that so many people came forward and introduced themselves as fellow Christians. One day they were delighted to see two members of the Indian team reading their Bibles and, to their surprise, discovered that they, too, were Christians.

The tour was an opportunity for quiet witness by the twins. Two other members of the team were active Christians; some were antagonistic, but most were interested and enjoyed the opportunity to talk about something other than cricket. 'What are you reading?' one of the team might ask when they saw the girls studying the Bible. 'This gave us an opening to talk about our faith and to discuss problems,' says Jill. 'Sometimes, when we were travelling, the others joined with us singing hymns and choruses; it helped all of us to keep going when we were weary. The tour was very tiring and, on occasions, very demanding on me as captain. I don't think I would have survived without my faith in Christ and the strength that comes through prayer. Prayer is the basis of my life and I always try to set aside a time for it. This is not always easy, and often it has to be on the coach while we are travelling between matches. I don't think that prayer should be confined to set times, however. Prayer should be spontaneous and on-going. For instance, I find I can be in a state of prayer even when I'm out on the cricket pitch, and I'm much more relaxed in consequence!'

Back in England, the twins received many invitations to speak to groups and meetings, to present awards and to be 'guest of honour' at various functions. Jill says, 'I'm doing things now I can't ever imagine doing before I became a Christian. If someone had told me six years ago that I would be standing up in a church talking about Jesus, I would have just laughed.'

At one of these meetings someone asked, 'How do you know that Christianity works?' Jill replied, 'It's a matter of acceptance. For instance, if you sit in an aeroplane, you accept the benefit of air conditioning, but how many of you know how it works? Jesus can work for you, he will be beneficial to your life, but just because you don't know *how* he works that doesn't mean you can't accept him. *You* have to make the choice to follow him, and then he reveals more and more to you. When you ask in faith, then he blesses you.'

Despite returning from India top of the bowling averages—taking 12 wickets from 21 overs—and consistently scoring the most runs in each of the trial matches preparing for the 1982 World Championship in New Zealand, Jill was left out of the England side. She accepted the disappointment philosophically. However, not going to New Zealand meant that she was able to take up a teaching post at a newly opened independent Christian school based at New Court Elim Church in Finsbury Park, London. It is now her church as well as her place of work. She says, 'It has given me much Christian teaching and Bible background. I've had time to get to grips with God's word.' This she values, as there was a period after leaving college when she had no regular church. While at the Hertfordshire sports centre she had experienced a conflict of priorities between the claims of God and sport. There had been a stage when she was unsure if she believed any more. 'But,' she recalls, 'there was no way God was going to let me go.' She made a second, more decisive commitment to Christ.

The twins have sometimes had to cope with a lack of understanding on the part of fellow Christians who find it hard to justify the time spent on what they consider 'leisure pursuits', particularly when it involves playing on Sunday. Jill says she has 'no qualms about it. I believe that every day of the week should be the same.'

Jane and Jill both think of the world of sport as a mission field. Although, at times, they have considered withdrawing from the sporting arena, they feel that God has called them to be in sport for a purpose. 'For instance,' Jill says, 'there are a lot of cricket people around whose only outlet in life is the sport, and whose friends are all cricket friends. There is nothing left for them after their playing days are over. There are some very nice people on a desperate pathway to nothing. If we take Christians off the sports field, those people are never going to know any different.'

Jane sums up the belief they share in the influence Christians can have in sport. 'Youngsters often admire sportspeople more than anyone else. They dream of becoming superstars. The girls want to be another Olga Korbut, the Russian gymnast, and the boys want to be a footballer like Kevin Keegan.' 'As far as playing is concerned,' says Jill, 'our aim is to do well whether we win or lose. There are, in fact, many ways in which the Christian life is like an athletic contest, but whereas there is usually only one winner in sport, *all* can be winners in the game of life.'

10: Dance on Ice

Nicky Slater: Ice Dance Champion

Born 6 April 1958

Nicholas Mark Slater had much to live up to. His parents, John and Joan, had been British amateur ice dance champions three times, runners up in the first two World Amateur Championships, and had gone on to win the World Professional title six times.

Nicky first went on the ice at the Manchester Ice Palace where his father and mother were skating instructors. He was only two and a half years old and, as he recalls, 'I was terrible!' It took him the next two and a half years to learn to stand up properly on his skates and not to skate on the side of his boots. When he was five, Nicky was given a weekly lesson with another instructor, but three years later his mother took over his training entirely.

His first ice dance partner was tiny, dark haired Anne Smyllie. Nicky says, 'I was madly in love with her and we made a cute duo.' When Anne outgrew him, Nicky who was then twelve, picked a pretty red-haired ten year old, Kathryn Winter. Three weeks later they took part in their first competition together and came fourth. They gradually became more confident and started to win open competitions, notably the Primary Championship in Nottingham in May 1971.

Nicky and Kathryn entered their first British Junior Championship in 1973. It was a significant event, not only because they came fourth, but also because the couple they beat into fifth place were Christopher Dean and his first partner, Sandra Elson. The following year after leading until the half-way stage, Nicky and Kathryn were placed second, and Chris and Sandra took the Junior title. For the next ten years Nicky was to find himself battling against Christopher Dean.

Skating was hard work. It involved getting up at 5am, practice from 6am to 8.30am, then off to school, sometimes skating in the lunch hour and again after school, and then there was homework still to be done, sometimes until 1am. 'It's why I didn't grow so tall,' Nicky says, 'I didn't have time to sleep long enough to grow tall!' In spite of the hours spent skating, when he eventually left school, Nikcy had obtained thirteen 'O' levels and three 'A' levels.

Seven months after the Junior Championship, Nicky and Kathryn took part in their first British Senior Championship. Although they were the youngest of the twelve couples competing, they were placed fifth. Meanwhile, Chris had acquired a new partner, Jayne Torvill. In one of their earliest encounters at the Bristol Ice Dance weekend, Nicky and Kathryn beat them into second place. The Nebelhorn Trophy held at Oberstdorf in the Bavarian Alps was Nicky and Kathryn's first international. There they discovered that the international judges have a preference for spectacular routines and showmanship, and they came a disappointing seventh out of twelve.

However, back home they were encouraged by an excellent fourth place in the British Senior Championship which led to their being named as reserves for the World Championship. Nicky recovered from a bout of glandular fever just in time to compete in the International Skating Union Junior Championships (now the Junior World Championships) held in France. He and Kathryn took first place. It was the proudest moment of their lives to date when they stood on the winners' podium and heard the British National Anthem played as the Union flag was raised.

Chris and Jayne were fast becoming a very effective partnership. Neverthless, in the 1976 British Senior Championship, Nicky and Kathryn were placed third and Chris and Jayne fourth. It was a good result especially as Nicky was under considerable strain at this time and not enjoying

136

skating as much as he had previously. His parents' marriage was crumbling, he was studying for school exams and he and Kathryn were constantly quarrelling. He knew he would have to find a new partner.

The girl he decided to ask was a slim athletic blonde named Karen Barber. Eventually she agreed and they commenced skating together on 31 May 1977. Their first major contest was to be the British Senior Championship in November. It was an event they nearly missed. Nicky had left school and was working in Manchester. A week before the championship, he stopped his motorcycle at some traffic lights. The lights changed to green and he moved off. A car coming from the opposite direction turned and hit him broadside on. Nicky recalls, 'I didn't even brake. I just relaxed and went into the air thinking, "I'm going to hurt myself when I land". Then everything stopped and I saw my helmet whizzing off down the road. My head was still on my shoulders, which was fine. I had my legs in the air and I was trying to feel which bits were broken, testing my arms and everything. I could move most things but my legs hurt a lot. When the ambulance came I remember thinking, "Oh God, Karen's going to be so disappointed we're not going to be able to skate the British".'

Fortunately, the crash bars on the sides of the bike prevented his legs from being crushed and Nicky was able to hobble out of hospital on crutches, his main injury being a badly brusied ankle. A week later Nicky and Karen took fourth place in the British Ice Championships. This time, however, they were beaten by Chris and Jayne, who were placed third and selected for the European and World Championship teams with Nicky and Karen first reserves.

Nicky and Karen's first win at an international was in February 1978 in Basle in Switzerland. Later, in the summer, they represented Britain again in the Nebelhorn Trophy in Oberstdorf, but were disappointed to take only fourth place. In November, in the British Championships, they had their best result to date—second place. The winners were Chris and Jayne, who took the title for the first time.

As a result of being runners-up in the British Championship, Nicky and Karen were selected as members of the national team for the 1979 European Championships in January where they came eleventh, and for the World Championships in March in which they were thirteenth out of twenty. Nicky continued to have problems with his injured ankle and, a month before the next British Championships, underwent an operation. Although not properly fit, he partnered Karen to another second place, with Chris and Jayne the winners. The championship was televised and, as a result, Nicky and Karen began to be recognised by people in the street. Sometimes this had embarrassing consequences, as Karen discovered when gingerly crossing an icy road, she slipped and fell just as a small girl shouted excitedly, 'Look, it's that ice skater'!

A creditable eighth out of fifteen in the 1980 European Championships in Gothenburg, was followed by a disappointing twelfth out of twelve in their Olympic debut at Lake Placid, in Canada! It was the first time Nicky had come last in a contest. He was sharing a room with Chris Dean in the Olympic village and when they arrived Nicky had put up a 'Snoopy' poster which read, 'The game is fun until you lose!' 'I got sick of looking at it,' says Nicky, 'it was so true!'

The World Championships followed in Dortmund where Nicky and Karen did better, coming tenth out of seventeen. A bronze medal in the British International which opened the 1980–81 season was followed by silver medals in the Skate Canada competition, the British Championship, and the NHK contest on the Japanese island of Sapporo. Chris and Jayne, who just missed the bronze medal in Dortmund, had been awarded a substantial grant by the Nottingham City Council which enabled them to give up their jobs and concentrate on skating. They could now afford to use the West German Training Centre at Oberstdorf where the facilities were far superior to anything available in Britain.

138

The difference this made was apparent when they took the gold medal at the 1981 European Championships in Innsbruck. Nicky and Karen, who had tried unsuccessfully to obtain a similar grant, nonetheless achieved their best result to date by finishing fifth out of nineteen. Predictably, the European gold medallists also won at the World Championships held in Hartford, USA. Nicky and Karen finished a well-deserved seventh out of twenty-one couples. Following an exhibition and teaching tour in China, they further enhanced their reputation in Britain by winning the prestigious John Davis Trophy.

Nicky, now twenty-three, and Karen twenty, decided to move to London where they could be coached by Jimmy Young at the Richmond ice rink. He saw them as a 'very nice, attractive, young-looking couple' and set out to give them a more mature and sophisticated look. At the beginning of the season, Chris and Jayne had decided that, outside England, they would take part only in the European and World Championships. Consequently, it was left to Nicky and Karen to uphold Britain's reputation in the other contests abroad. In the Skate America competition they won the bronze medal and had their third international win in the NHK contest in Japan. Meanwhile, at the British Championship, Chris and Jayne retained the title in a flurry of maximum marks, while Nicky and Karen came second for the fourth time. The 1982 European and World Championships were equally frustrating when they could do no better than the previous year, with fifth and seventh places respectively.

Nicky and Karen were still having financial problems, although they were now receiving a small grant from the Sports Aid Foundation and some help from the British Skating Association. Jimmy Young not only gave much of his coaching time free but sometimes had to sponsor them himself when finances were critical. There was very little time for social life and all their friends were fellow skaters. However, they did become involved in helping charitable causes whenever possible. While they skated in Altrincham they were associated with a school for the mentally handicapped. In London they took part on the St. Stephen's radio at the Westminster Children's Hospital and at the Great Ormond Street Hospital. They have also done projects for the Sports Aid Foundation and performed each year in the Muscular Dystrophy Gala at Solihull, as well as befriending and helping handicapped individuals.

The 1982–83 season was to prove Nicky and Karen's most successful to date, although it had its disappointments, too. Jimmy Young sought to give them a new and more lively image for their dance routines. They also ventured into comedy with an exhibition number skated to the music 'New Fangled Tango' which proved extremely popular with audiences everywhere. In the first competition of the season, the St. Ivel International, they were again second, this time to the Americans, Judy Blumberg and Michael Seibert. Following the St Ivel, they went to Holland where they won the Ennia Cup, beating the Russian pair, Sergei Ponomarenko and Marina Klimova. It was their fourth international win. Back home for the British Championship they were runners-up for a record fifth year.

However, before the European Championship Jayne Torvill fell in practice and damaged her shoulder. As a result, she and Chris had to withdraw, and Nicky and Karen went as the leading British ice dance pair. Needless to say the pressure not to let anyone down was so intense that they failed to skate their best, finishing with the bronze medal, behind the two Russian couples. Despite everything Karen and Nicky established themselves in the affection of the British television audience by their sporting acceptance of defeat.

At the World Championships, Nicky made a spectacular entrance on the warm up when he stepped on the ice without removing his skate guards and fell flat on his face! They were doing well until the highlight of their OSP (Original Set Pattern) when, right in front of the judges, Nicky fell and sat on Karen! It was their first fall in competition in the six years they had been together. Nicky seemed completely dazed and could hardly carry on, and they were placed eighth in the OSP and finished fifth overall.

In preparation for the Olympic season, their coach decided to try something which no-one else had yet attempted—to bring humour into an entire championship routine. For the free dance they hit on the idea of Charlie Chaplin on ice, re-creating the situations and atmosphere of the old black and white silent films. Nicky and Karen were very excited about the routine, but at its preview for the National Skating Association, some of the British officials criticised it for being too 'exhibition-like'. This was very disheartening, but it was too late to make any fundamental changes before the competitive season began.

The first public showing of their new routines was at the St Ivel International in September. After the compulsory dances and the OSP Nicky and Karen were lying second behind the Americans, Richard Dalley and Carol Fox, a couple they had never beaten. The final result depended on the free dance; they were very nervous. As they entered they received a thunderous ovation from the packed audience. Richard and Carol skated after them and Nicky and Karen assumed that, as on previous occasions, the American couple would win. To their delight, they themselves were announced the winners, the success of their Chaplin routine had earned them the vital marks. It was their fifth international win, but the first one in front of a home crowd, and it was a high moment for them both.

After their success at the St Ivel, Nicky went through an adverse reaction. He became very depressed at the likelihood of coming second yet again at the forthcoming British Championship. To make matters worse he fell over in practice. He recalls, 'I wasn't going very fast. I just went plop on my back, a dead fall. They say when you're feeling down that any injury becomes even worse, and I had really hurt myself, putting four vertebrae out, and for a while I couldn't move at all.' Nicky knew that he had been injured too badly to have any real chance in the Championship but he was afraid to withdraw in case it was seen as an excuse to avoid another defeat by Chris and Jayne. Nicky forced himself back on the ice but fell again in practice and could not skate at all in the week before the contest. On the night of the Championships he was in great pain as he went through the compulsories and then he had a bad fall in the OSP. During the interval, before the free dance, one of the officials told him, 'If you can't do it properly, you shouldn't do it.' This advice made it easier for them to pull out.

In spite of their withdrawal, they were selected for the Olympic team subject to a later fitness test. A visit to an osteopath eventually put right Nicky's spine and they were fit to take part in the European Championships early in January 1984. This time it was Karen's turn to suffer an injury. After hurting her knee in the OSP she bravely skated the free dance with her leg strapped from ankle to thigh. She managed to complete the Championship and they were placed fourth overall.

At the Olympics in Sarajevo, Nicky and Karen, although skating well, were placed sixth. In the World Championships in Ottawa their new OSP was well received and, at that stage, they were lying fifth. For the free dance, they had to follow Chris and Jayne's sensational 'Bolero' for which they had received a record number of maximum marks. Nicky recalls, 'After all the sixes flashed up, as we stepped onto the ice, Chris and Jayne came over to wish us luck. It was a special moment and we felt very proud. Chris and Jayne realised that they had gone as far as they could go and were moving on to conquer new worlds and there were we, the upstarts, ready to take over upholding British tradition, and they were supporting us.' In spite of the rapturous reception of 'Bolero', the audience gave Nicky and Karen a standing ovation for their Chaplin routine and booed the judges when they marked them fifth in this section and fifth overall. Nicky comments, 'I knew that it was the best we'd ever performed and that was the most important thing.'

With Chris and Jayne having turned professional, Nicky and Karen were now Britain's leading ice dance skaters and knew they must produce something very special for the 1984–85 season. With the World Championship taking place in Tokyo they felt that they should do something oriental for the all important free dance. The first problem was to find the right music. After a fruitless search they were put in touch with Mike Batt, who had composed 'Bright Eyes' for the film 'Watership Down'. Nicky and Karen had always dreamed of having music specially written for them and, to their delight, Mike agreed to produce a kind of oriental Romeo and Juliet score. David and Elizabeth Emanuel, fashion designers to Princess Diana, designed costumes for their OSP and free dance routines. The free dance outfits were particularly striking with wide shoulders which sparkled with diamanté and had dragons embroidered with gold thread. Both the music and their dance was named 'Dragon Dance'.

In October, after years of financial struggle, ITV granted Nicky and Karen some substantial help. Although there were only five weeks before the British Championships, it enabled them to go to Oberstdorf for some concentrated training. Even then, their practice had to be interrupted for a flying visit back to England to skate in front of the Queen and Prince Philip in the opening gala for the Gillingham ice rink. However, they felt it was worth it just to be presented to the Queen and the Prince after the show.

The long awaited day of the Championship arrived. Nicky felt fairly calm, Karen very nervous. Ten minutes before they were due to go on the ice, a large bouquet was delivered to Karen. It was from Jayne Torvill, who had signed the card herself, wishing them luck. Following the compulsory and OSP, in which they felt they had done well, Nicky and Karen changed into their spectacular Dragon Dance costumes. As they were going out for their warm up, Nicky noticed that the clip at the back of Karen's headband was coming undone. The free dance was a critical part of the contest and nothing could be allowed to go wrong. A television crew were filming nearby and Nicky asked desperately if anyone had a pair of pliers. One of the crew leapt forward and hastily fixed the clasp. For Nicky and Karen the big moment had come. The atmosphere was electric and the audience responded enthusiastically to their performance. First place in the free dance gave them first place overall. They could hardly believe that they were the new British champions. Nicky recalls, 'We claimed the British title on Friday 16th November 1984, a day that will always burn brightly in our minds. For six seemingly endless years we had lived in the shadow of Jayne Torvill and Christopher Dean.'

Nicky and Karen followed their British success with a sixth consecutive victory in the Japanese NHK contest and after some exhibition skating, began preparation for the European and World Championships. As the European approached they both felt increasingly apprehensive. The British public, used to the success of Chris and Jayne, expected Nicky and Karen to repeat the same victories in international competition. The pressure of such high expectation made them over-anxious and this undoubtedly affected their performance.

They missed the European bronze medal by a very marginal five to four decision in which a tenth of a point would have tipped the scales in their favour. They were bitterly disappointed but tried not to show it. Nicky comments, 'Afterwards we decided there was no point in being gloomy. We've got to learn to take the knocks. But it did hurt and we were afraid we'd let people down.' Many of those watching felt that the judging had been unfair and Nicky and Karen received much sympathetic appreciation. Nicky remembers, 'We said to ourselves, "Okay, we've been run over, but we can't just sit down and take it. We really have to work hard and show them." We were really bucked up by a letter sent to us by a girl who was going to do her 'O' levels and was sure she was going to fail. She was so depressed that she was even contemplating suicide. Then she saw how we handled our defeat. She wrote that because of the way we'd stood up and said we'd go on fighting, she decided even if she didn't pass she was going to go on fighting too. It made us feel that everything we'd done was worthwhile, at a point when we felt nothing was going right.' Another young, disabled girl sent them a medal she had won for horseriding. It was to make up for Nicky and Karen not having won a medal themselves in the European Championships. They were deeply touched.

The World Championships followed in Tokyo and Nicky and Karen were placed sixth, once more losing a place to the German couple by a five to four decision. They were at a cross-roads in their career. Nicky sums up how they felt after this second disappointing international result, 'After the emotional range of feelings we'd gone through that season we were absolutely exhausted. We had no reserves whatever to call on and that made it even harder for us to decide whether we would continue in amateur competition.'

Originally, Nicky and Karen had planned to continue as amateurs for at least one more season. Now they were not so sure. Jimmy Young, their coach, felt that the time had come to turn professional. Nicky and Karen had some discussions with Robin Cousins about the possibility of joining the 'Ice Majesty' show. When this came to nothing he tried hard to prepare some new material with which to defend their British title. However, Karen told Nicky she did not want to continue competing and would like to join her friend Jayne in the Torvill and Dean 'World Tour'. Nicky did not feel the show was right for him, and they went through a period of intense soul-searching. Usually it was Nicky who made the decisions. But in this instance, it was Karen who brought the matter to a head by announcing her intention to turn professional and to join the 'World Tour'. On 26 August, in an interview on ITV, they broke the news that they were parting. It was a time of great sadness for them both, and for the British public, who had such high hopes of them as the natural successors to Chris and Jayne.

Looking back, Nicky says, 'I wish we could have carried on together either as amateurs or professionals. It would have been difficult, but with the backing we were now receiving from ITV, I feel we could have done much better in competition. Having said that, there's the text, "All things work together for good to them that love God", and I'm sure that, when we look back, everything will have turned out for the best.'

During these months of indecision, two other life-changing events had taken place for Nicky. He had become a committed Christian and had fallen in love. As a child, Nicky had been taught by his father to say his prayers and he went to Sunday School until he was nine. However, it was not until his early twenties that he began to think seriously about religion. He says 'There were lots of times when we were skating when I felt really lousy and I wanted to go into a church and say a prayer, but then you felt guilty because the only times you wanted to do that were when things were tough and not when they were good; so I didn't. That went on for quite a while. Then, when I was in America, feeling very dissatisfied with my skating performance, I went into a bookshop and picked up a book by Norman Vincent Peale called, *The Power of Positive Thinking*. I thought it was a business book, but when I went through it I found it was all about the Bible, taking little quotes and applying them to everyday living. I was struck by Paul's words, "I can do all things through Christ who strengthens me", and "if God be for us who can be against us?" The book suggested that you write down the texts and carry them with you. I did this for a time and then let it slide. But it got me thinking about religion.

'Then I came back to England. It was Christmas '84, and I met a girl that I had not seen for three years. I asked, "What's happened to you since we last met?" She said, "Nothing much, apart from the fact I've become a Christian." I asked all sorts of questions about what she meant and what had happened. Eventually, it led to me going along to her house group and asking a lot more difficult questions. The folk there suggested I go to the local church in Richmond. The next Sunday I actually got to the doors of Duke Street Baptist Church, but hadn't the courage to go in, and walked away. The following week when I went along I was late and I had to sit right at the front. The preacher was Stanley Voke and a lot of what he said seemed to really make sense, I felt as though I'd been run over by a truck! I talked to him afterwards and that was it. I expected all sorts of bright lights and fireworks to go up but they didn't! But, everything really started from there. I said the words of commitment, I felt their meaning and wanted them to be true, but at that point I didn't really understand about Jesus and about Him being alive and so on. I knew I had a long way to go.

'A few days later, I went to Duke Street to find my wallet which I thought I had left there. They were having a Business Men's Lunch and I got myself invited. I sat next to David Shafik who invited me home and he and his family have been incredibly helpful and supportive to me. As a new Christian I needed someone to guide me and it was as if he had been nominated!' In June, Nicky was invited to a 'Christians in Sport' service at the Millmead Centre, Guildford. After the service, he was sitting next to Cliff Richard, signing autographs. 'I noticed this vivacious blonde and was captivated. Our eyes met. It took me four times walking past her to pluck up courage to say "hello". I asked her out to dinner and, to my surprise, she said "yes". Her name was Jo McGirr and although she had a dim memory of our Chaplin number, she wasn't a follower of skating and it was refreshing to talk to someone away from the sport.' Jo had been a committed Christian for some years and was able to help Nicky as he learned to pray and read the Bible and to work through some of the questions that his enquiring mind raised. He was baptised on 15 September 1985 and he and Jo were married on 12 October.

Nicky is very honest about his progress in the Christian faith. He says, 'There have been very tough times when you have to rely on God's help but when things are going better you tend to forget, although I do try not to. I don't always read the Bible as regularly as I should. I always pray and it's amazing some of the things that have happened when I've asked for help. It's difficult having been in the public eye. Sometimes, because of who you are, you are put on a pedestal, but I know I'm not an ideal example of what a Christian person should be. I'm very young as a Christian but I want to learn more and know more. I'd like to get more involved in the church and do more. I helped with a children's holiday Bible club during the summer. It was a lot of fun and I learned a lot from it. Being a Christian makes things much better, but in some ways much harder. I know how I should be but that doesn't make it any easier to be like that. It's an ongoing battle.' Life was very different after the break up of the skating partnership. Nicky says, 'From jetting around the world, living between 5–star hotels and bed-sits, just enjoying skating, and then suddenly to be married, living a normal life seemed very strange. The skating stopped, something I'd been doing all my life. Normally, you would join a show, but I was now without a skating partner. I did get a 'partner' of a sort. I had a full sized dummy made, we called her Doris. She cost over £2,000 but I only used her for some seven shows as she was too heavy and she couldn't stand up on her own! I also did a few skating shows, commentating for television and some appearances in schools.

'Then "Sport Aid" came along. In the aftermath of Bob Geldoff's "Band Aid" and "Live Aid" which raised millions of pounds for the starving people of the world it was decided to get together a skating gala for the Band Aid Trust. One day, a guy phoned me up and said, "We've got this show booked for May 24 at the National Exhibition Centre in Birmingham, would you like to produce it?" I said, "Yes, great," thinking "what do I have to do as a producer?" What it entailed was putting together a complete skating production in seven weeks. At the start all we had was the ice and a general agreement with some of the skaters, although some of them were about to pull out. I had to persuade the skaters, sort out the show's format, the choreography, music, lighting, and stage management, as well as negotiate with sponsors and television. In the middle of the first performance the television people threatened to walk out because the lighting was inadequate. We worked to improve it, but then there was nothing more that could be done. They were getting more and more angry with me. I retired to the loo and prayed for help! I'm sure it was in answer to prayer that I was able to keep very calm and, in the end, the lighting proved adequate and the one-hour television show was a huge success.

'We had probably the greatest collection of skating people that has ever been brought together at one time. The star line up included Robin Cousins, Scott Hamilton, Debbie Thomas and, of course, Chris and Jayne. Karen and I did our 'Tango' routine. I was far from fit and we only had four days to practise, but the response of the crowd was tremendous. However, the next day I could hardly walk! 8,000 people attended each of the two performances and over £1,000,000 was raised from the skating alone. I wanted it to be a joyful yet thoughtful occasion because we were there for a purpose. I think the message came across. For me, it was probably the greatest thing I've ever achieved.'

What of the future? Nicky is in the process of setting up a business, 'The Spice Organisation Ltd (SPecially for ICE)', a management and consultancy service concerned with ice sport and leisure activities. Nicky says, 'We hope to be producing big events with skating included in them and to get involved in the ownership, management and operation of centres where skating takes place. There is a real lack of ice rinks and training facilities in this country and we want to encourage more people to skate. It's very much a learning experience for me, but very exciting. I still hope that when the business is established, Karen and I will be able to skate together again, doing exhibitions and competitions around the world, not as a thing that has to be done to survive but as something we do because we enjoy entertaining people. That would be the ideal. Of course, people may not want to come and see us in a couple of years time, but I hope they will!

'In the meantime, since becoming a Christian, I am discovering that when things seem to be going wrong, it's the Lord saying "lean on me". That's what Jo and I try to do. We know he is going to provide.'

For further reading:

Spice on Ice: Karen Barber and Nicky Slater with Sandra Stevenson, Sidgwick & Jackson Ltd, 1985.

11: Black Flash

Carl Lewis: Olympic Quadruple Gold Medallist

Born 1 July 1961

'Carl Lewis stands quietly at the end of the plywood runway, eyeing the sand of the long jump pit 160 feet away. He is priming himself for his last jump in the Millrose Games, and he needs to leap at least 27 feet 6 inches (8.41m.), to keep his string of long jump victories alive. He tenses. His sister, Carol, braces her feet against some loose planking on the runway to keep Carl's Nikes from slipping on takeoff, as they did on his previous attempts.

Suddenly he bursts forward. His legs and arms churn harmoniously as he accelerates. His shoes become a red-and-white blur blazing down the plywood. Faster and faster he runs until it seems that he'll dive right into the pit. But just a hairbreadth before he does, Carl plants his right foot and launches his 6–foot–2, 175–pound body into the air.

His legs and arms begin windmilling like a man who's suddenly had his bicycle yanked from beneath him. On and on he sails over the brown sand. Finally gravity reasserts its force and brings him back to earth—but not before he's hurled himself more than a foot beyond his nearest competitor's mark.

Jubilantly Carl leaps from the sand, fists thrust skyward. His sister clasps him in a bear hug as the Madison Square Gardens crowd cheers. The PA system blares the announcement that Carl has just jumped 28 feet 10¼ inches (8.82m.)—setting a new world indoor record by nine inches. Experts agree that the jump, which equalled Carl's best outdoor effort, would have to be converted to 30 feet

(9.17m.) outdoors. Both marks are second only to Bob Beamon's 1968 world record of 29 feet 2½ inches, set at an altitude of 7,400 feet in Mexico City—aided by a four mile an hour wind.'*

Frederick Carlton Lewis is generally acknowledged to be the finest sprinter and long jumper since the legendary Jesse Owens, the black athlete who won four gold medals at the 1936 Olympic Games in Berlin. He is described in the magazine 'The Runner' (October 1984) as 'not merely a great athlete, but the great athelete by which other athletes are to be measured.'

Carl was the third of four children born and brought up in the Philadelphia suburb of Willingboro, New Jersey. Apart from a fine physique, he has the advantage of coming from a very athletic family. His parents were both athletics coaches and former runners and jumpers. His eldest brother, Mackie, was a county sprint record holder, his middle brother, Cleve, was a top soccer player in the North American Soccer League and his younger sister, Carol, is the current US Women's Long Jump record holder and bronze medallist in the 1983 World Championships.

In their childhood, Carl and Carol used to build sand castles in a long jump pit and then jump into them, seeing how many they could knock down. When, at the age of ten, Carl heard of Bob Beamon's world record jump, he borrowed a tape measure from his father and measured out the distance in his front yard. 'It looked like two Cadillacs,' he says, 'I couldn't believe anyone could jump that far.' By a happy coincidence, when he was twelve, he won a regional long jump title and was presented with the trophy by Jesse Owens himself. Recognising his talent, Owens told him,

*Gary Kauffman reporting in *Athletes in Action* (Summer 1984). This and quotations from interviews first published in the Spring '83 and Summer '84 editions of the magazine are published with permission. Some other brief quotations are from *Track and Field News* and *The Runner*

'You sure are determined. You're a small youngster among giants.' Within a few years that 'small youngster' was being described as 'the second Jesse Owens'.

Carl claims to have 'lived, eaten and slept athletics' since he was seven. At the University of Houston he majored in Communications and Broadcasting. Here he came under the influence of two men who have played a very important part in his development as an athlete. Clyde Duncan, Houston's sprint coach, helped Carl to 'look beyond himself and to think positively.' University athletics coach, Tom Tellez, who has remained Carl's coach, concentrated on his physical development. Tellez was greatly impressed with his flat-out speed, an essential requisite for a successful long jumper, and with his guidance Carl's technique, both as a jumper and sprinter, showed marked improvement.

Carl has not lost in any outdoor long jump event since 1980, or any indoor long jump since 1981. As a junior athlete he was well above average, but he really established his reputation in June 1981 at the TAC* US National Championships at Sacramento. In the qualifying round of the long jump, the twenty year old university student made an astonishing leap of 8.73 metres. But for a too strong following wind, this would have ranked as a new low altitude world record. In the final, Carl reached 8.62 metres with his opening jump. This was the world's second best jump of all time and the longest without the assistance of the thin air of high altitude.

Carl then crossed the stadium for the 100 metres final. He started slowly, accelerating about 60 metres into the race, 'At 80 metres it was all over and I smiled as I took the lead,' he said. He won comfortably in 10.13 sec. Carl returned to the long jump pit, prepared to jump again, but it was not necessary. The previous year's winner, Larry Myricks, finished with a leap of 8.45 metres, 0.17 metres

*The Athletics Congress—the US Governing Body of Track and Field Athletics.

behind Carl's winning jump. Nobody had won both the short sprint and the long jump at a US national championship since Jesse Owens, forty-five years previously.

The same year, at a sports meeting in Dallas, Carl ran the 100 metres in 10.00 sec., the fastest-ever without altitude assistance. At the end of the season, Carl assessed his progress. '1981 was a year for me to establish myself on a world-class level as the No. 1 sprinter and long jumper, and to set some goals that seemed unattainable to others, but that I thought were quite attainable.' Carl was deservedly voted 'Track and Field News' Athlete of the Year.

Another significant event of a different kind took place during the year when Carl was competing at the NCAA* Track and Field Championships in Baton Rouge, LA. One evening, Carl's friend, Willie Gault, a notable sprinter and high hurdler, invited him to a meeting in another room of the motel where they were staying. The speaker was Dr Sam Mings, the man who had led Willie to Christ. Formerly a businessman, now an evangelist, Sam Mings founded and heads 'Lay Witnesses for Christ Evangelistic Association', which he describes as a 'soul-winning ministry reaching across all denominations and racial barriers'. That night, Carl and two hundred other athletes heard Dr Mings speak on the subject, 'Jesus Christ—man's only hope'. He went on to explain the basic principles involved in beginning a personal relationship with Christ and concluded with a challenge to commitment.

Carl's parents, both Christians, had brought up their children to know about God and to go to church. Carl had heard such a message many times before. But now, for the first time, he began to realise that he needed to take some personal action in response. He returned the next evening and, at the invitation of Dr Mings, asked Christ to come into his life. 'I was always surrounded by a religious environment,' Carl recalls, 'but I hadn't actually made any

*National Collegiate Athletic Association.

kind of commitment. I made that commitment that night, because I felt some voids in my life and I knew they needed to be filled with the Lord.'

The next day, Carl brought his brothers and sister to hear Sam Mings. Like Carl, they hesitated and then returned the following evening to make decisions for Christ.

During the five-day series of evangelistic meetings at the NCAA Championships, Dr. Mings reports that 78 all-American athletes, some of them world record holders, received Christ as their Saviour and Lord. Carl joined several other leading athletes in signing an assignment committing themselves to three or four weeks of witnessing each year with 'Lay Witnesses for Christ'. Sam Mings says, 'Carl is one of 4000 very visible athletic stars who are encouraged to use their platform in life to point those who look to them to the "True Star"—Jesus Christ'. Carl has since increased his commitment by joining the steering committee and, more recently, the executive committee of 'Lay Witnesses for Christ'.

The 'voids' Carl had felt in his life were filled. 'Since then', he says, 'I've been more at ease with the way I act and react, and I've been more comfortable about everyday life and how to deal with it'. Christ became more important than anything else in his life and each day bacame more satisfying and fulfilling.

The following year, 1982, now representing the Californ-ian based Santa Monica Track Club, Carl again ran 100 metres in 10 sec (9.9 sec manual timing). He also extended his range of events to include the 200 metres, and very soon had returned an outstanding time of 20.27 sec. In addition, at the US Sports Festival held at Indianapolis in July, he improved his distance in the long jump to a remarkable 8.76 metres. He was drawing very close to Beamon's 'unbreakable' altitude record of 8.90 metres at the 1968 Olympics.

Carl had begun to set goals for himself in high school—one had been to jump over 7.62 metres, a distance he achieved as a freshman at the University of Houston.

To attain new goals in track and field, he trains up to two hours a day, concentrating on weight training and technique in the autumn and running in the spring, with a full competitive programme in the summer. He admits to being a 'chronic workaholic', but says that God has guided him through friends to change his work habits. They have also helped him deal with the pressure which fame inevitably brings. 'The pressures that I face most are from people commanding my time,' says Carl. 'When it happens, I now sit back ask for time and pray to the Lord.'

No matter how busy, Carl still makes time to offer encouragement to others. He recalls how he was able to help a high jumper overcome a frustrating setback. 'At the time he was No. 1 in the world,' he says, 'At this particular meet, he had two misses at a low height, so he was very confused. All I did was to sit down and pray and while we were praying together, I was able to settle him down, and he went on to win the competition.'

That same summer, Carl won the TAC titles in both the 100 metres and long jump and, for the second year running, was named Athlete of the Year by *Track and Field News*. However, although he was top ranked in the world's best at the long jump and short sprint, so far, all he had to show for it in *world* terms was a win in the long jump in the Rome World Cup of 1981.

Although Carl had the 1984 Olympic Games as his main athletic goal, he reached peak form in the 1983 US outdoor TAC Championships in June. He became the first athlete in 97 years to win three national titles. He started by winning the 100 metres for the third consecutive year. His other events were on the last day of the meeting; the long jump came first. Carl stripped off his tracksuit to make his initial leap. He hoped that it would be long enough to win him the event. He was due to compete in the semi-finals and finals of the 200 metres within the following two hours, and had planned to return to his hotel to rest.

The weather was warm and overcast. Carl hurtled down the runway, took off at some 27 mph, cycled in the air and landed in a spurt of sand. A roar went up from the crowd as the distance appeared on the score board—8.79 metres—it was the longest jump ever made at sea level. He was so pleased that, instead of returning to the hotel he decided to jump again, attempting an absolute world record. This time he reached 8.71 metres; although not as good as his first jump, it was long enough to win him the competition. He put on his grey tracksuit, passed his four remaining jumps, and lay on his stomach to watch the other competitiors. It was the third consecutive year he had won the national long jump championship.

A little later, Carl went out on the track and won the 200 metre semi-finals. In the final he amazed everyone by clocking 19.75 sec., whilst easing up and raising both arms aloft. That gesture must have had a braking effect which cost him Pietro Mennea's altitude record of 19.72 sec. It was however, a new *low altitude* US and World Record.

In all three events Carl had demolished class fields of Olympic calibre. It was no surprise, therefore, when later that year, he ran the 100 metres in 9.93sec. Unfortunately, this could not count as a record as it was wind assisted. He also ran a 9.97 sec 100 metres which *was* ratified as a non-altitude World Record, a time which can be said to outrank Calvin Smith's 9.93 sec world best which was achieved in the thin air of high altitude.

Carl arrived at the firs IAAF* World Championships held in August at Helsinki, as the man everyone most wanted to see. As expected, he took the 100 metres title and the crowd waited expectantly for his appearance in the long jump. Would Bob Beamon's thin air 8.90 metres leap be surpassed? The stewards allowed Carl to delay his first attempt in order to anchor the US sprint relay team in a semi-final victory. Carl returned to the jump pit. The spectators clapped rhythmically as he pounded down the runway. They fell silent as he sprang from the take-off

*International Amateur Athletics Federation.

board, threw himself forward and performed a pedalling, double-hitch kick before landing.

In the infield the rotating scoreboard lit up 892. The crowd gasped, but before they could cheer what appeared to be a new world record, an accompanying number was displayed on the board: 8.55. A groan of disappointment arose as it became clear that the figure had been Carl's number as a competitor, and 8.55 the length of his jump. Nonetheless, that first leap was good enough to take the most predictable medal of the Games. It was also one better than the winning leap of Lutz Dombrowski from East Germany in the 1980 Moscow Olympics at which the United States did not compete for political reason.

Without troubling to jump again, Carl returned to the track for the 4 x 100 metres relay final. Emmit King, Willie Gault and Calvin Smith ran at a blistering pace to hand Carl the baton with a fractional lead over the Russians and Italians. Carl switched the baton from left hand to right and, accelerating away from the field behind, flashed across the finish line four yards clear of Piettro Mennea, Italy's Olympic 200 metre champion. The time, 37.86 sec, was a new world record, the American team being the first quartet to complete the distance under 38 seconds.

The achievement of the four black athletes was more than just a victory for their country. All four men are committed Christians and members of 'Lay Witnesses for Christ'. Immediately after the race, out on the track, they linked arms and bowed their heads in a prayer of gratitude for what they regarded as a spiritual victory. Willie Gault, who finished third in the 100 metre high hurdles, and now plays professional American Football for the Chicago Bears, serves as the Chairman of the 'Lay Witnesses' steering committee for athletes' involvement. He was one of those who had talked with Carl before he committed his life to Christ. 'It's a good feeling to help someone, and I'm glad to be an ambassador for God,' Willie says.

With three gold medals, two won within fifty-five minutes, and a share in the world record performance in the relay, Carl was undoubtedly the supreme athlete of the inaugural World Championships. He took patriotic pride in his achievement. 'This is the first time I've ever been in an international competition when I could stand on the podium, see our flag flying and hear our national anthem,' he says. Yet he confesses to a higher loyalty than patriotism, 'Ultimately, I've got only one person to answer to, and that's my Lord'. For an unprecedented third consecutive year, Carl was declared *Track and Field News* Athlete of the Year.

Naturally, Carl's fame has resulted in a constant demand for interviews and speaking engagements. 'At least ten foreign countries have called wanting me for an 'Athlete of the Year' banquet or award ceremony,' says Carl. Although he finds it difficult to say 'no', it is impossible to work, train, compete and fill all these demands. Nonetheless, like his childhood idol, Jesse Owens, he wants his admiring public to know about his decision for Christ. 'I like being known as a Christian,' he says, 'because it brings a lot of good feelings, encouragement and letters from people that I didn't get before I prayed to receive Christ as my personal Saviour.'

Carl seeks to apply his Christian principles to the world of athletics. 'One of the biggest concerns in sports is the uncertainty of the outcome,' he says. 'Now I'm able to do my best and not to worry about the outcome. If I know I've given my all for my Lord and Saviour, that's all I can do. I don't have to worry about it—win, lose or draw.' He readily acknowledges that neither he nor his accomplishments control his life. 'I do love the Lord,' he says, 'and he's the most important person in my life.'

Because of his relaxed and confident attitude to life, the media has sometimes accused Carl of arrogance. His coach, Tom Tellez, defends him, saying, 'Carl is very, very confident of what he can do and what his abilities are. At the same time, he is the most un-arrogant person I know. Confident, yes. Arrogant no. Anyone who says he is arrogant, doesn't really know him.'

Gary Kauffman is another who declares that fame has not inflated Carl's ego. He writes, 'He smiles easily, is friendly and courteous to everyone and would probably fulfill every request for an interview or public appearance if Joe Douglas didn't say "no" for him. And he hates to hurt anyone's feelings. But lately it's been Carl's feelings that have been hurt. A naturally enthusiastic person, he usually reacts to a victory with raised arms and hugs—an ordinary reaction for his outstanding performances. But competitors have viewed such actions with a jaundiced eye, labelling him a showboat. One critic said, "There'll be some serious celebrating when Carl gets beat." Such criticisms shocked Carl. He sought counsel with Sam Mings, who advised, "Keep your eyes on the Lord." Sam reminded Carl that he was competing to please God first. Other friends in the Lay Witnesses for Christ movement also offered encouragement. "At first, I felt saddened by the criticisms," Carl says. "In sports, fans look up to us a lot. The press is very hard on athletes, and, of course, they're very vocal. But the only vocal ones who can make a big difference are the athletes, and when they say negative things or when his fellow competitors pick sour grapes, Carl's faith helps him. "I cannot control what other people think of me,", he says. "I just need to fulfil myself in Jesus Christ to be the best possible person I can be." '

At the 1984 Olympic Games held in Los Angeles, Carl was very much the focus of attention as so many followers of athletics expected him to emulate Jesse Owens's quadruple success at the 1936 Games. Carl had set himself the same goal but was not unduly worried by the world's expectations, as he finds he gains energy from the public and their hopes. He says, 'I have always been, and always will be, the type of person who wants more; and, on the outside, what other people call pressure, I call inspiration. That's my way of motivating myself'.

In the 100 metres, Carl had no difficulty in winning the two heats and semi-final that took him into the final. The reigning Olympic Champion, Alan Wells of Great Britain, handicapped by a swollen right foot, was eliminated in the semi-final, but Carl faced strong opposition as the eight finalists crouched on their starting blocks. Following a false start, it was fellow American, Sam Graddy, and Ben Johnson of Canada, who were away the fastest, and they held a clear lead at halfway. From that point Carl began to close on them and by 70 metres he was moving away with every stride. He tore across the finishing line with arms held high in jubilation. His time was 9.99 sec, and he finished 0.2 sec (or nearly 2½m.) clear of Graddy, the widest winning margin in the history of the Olympic short sprint. Commenting on the race, Carl said, 'I got a good start tonight, but some of the others got out faster. Once I started to come on at about 50 metres I relaxed and felt very confident.' He also told reporters, 'As far as I'm concerned, 60 per cent of it is over. This is by far the toughest event for me, because so much can go wrong. That's why I got so emotional when I won, because it was the most difficult of the four events in which I'm competing. Now it's one down and three to go.'

The next day Carl prepared the ground for a second gold medal when he qualified for the Long Jump final with a casual wind-assisted leap of 8.30 metres. Only three others topped 8 metres.

A busy day followed with Carl strolling through his heat in the first round of the 200 metres in the second-slowest winning time of 21.02 sec. In the second round he ran into the wind to clock a faster winning time of 20.48 sec. Next was the final of the Long Jump. Carl limited his exertions to an opening leap of 8.54 metres into the wind followed by a no-jump. That first jump was good enough to win him the Gold medal and, to the disappointment of the crowd, he passed up his remaining four jumps. Some of the 90,000 spectators in the Coliseum booed when they realised that he was not going on to attack Beamon's world record. Carl explained afterwards that his hamstring was tight after the two rounds of the 200 metres earlier in the day and was stiffening by his second jump. 'I didn't want to risk anything,' he said. 'The world record can be broken, but records are not uppermost in my mind—I just want to win. Competition is the foremost thing to me, competition and the fun of it. Everything else comes after.'

Having won two gold medals and with the world's secular news media pressing for interviews, Carl slipped away to take part in a television programme beamed to the nation by satellite from the First Baptist Church of Van Nuys. There were those who were surprised that Carl should break his concentration on the athletic events still to come, but he was determined to be with the other top Olympians who were to be interviewed on a special programme, 'Three Hours with the Stars'. Dr Jess Moody hosting the show said, 'I believe the greatest spiritual awakening taking place in the US is among the athletes. Half of our US track team are born again evangelical Christians who are not ashamed to talk about Christ.'

Following a musical programme, the audience stood and applauded as Carl appeared on stage. 'Because Jesus is number one in our lives, we're beginning to stand up for Him more,' Carl told the crowd. 'It's been a great Olympics, but this year has probably been the most trying year of my entire life, career-wise. And, more than any other year, I've realised how important Jesus Christ is to my life.'

'My preparation for everything I've done has revolved around Him. When track and field and the medals are forgotten, Jesus Christ will still be Lord. I hope all of you who have prayed to receive Jesus Christ will be very happy. All of you who have not yet received Him, I hope you will. He is the only One who will be there. . . . today. . . . tomorrow. . . . forever!'

The final of the 200 metres took place the next day. Carl ran a very fast bend to lead by 2 metres at the 100 mark and held that lead to cross the line, ahead of his team-mates, Kirk Baptiste and Thomas Jefferson. 'Today was special', said Carl, 'because I looked back at the finish and saw two other Americans right behind me.' His winning

162

time of 19.80 sec was a new Olympic record and the third fastest ever 200 metres. It was also probably the finest run of all time at that distance, for Pietro Mennea's world record of 19.72 sec was set at high altitude, Carl's own sea-level best of 19.75 sec had a 1.5m. tailwind, on this occasion in Los Angeles, there was an 0.9m. *headwind.*

The US team of Sam Graddy, Ron Brown, Calvin Smith and Carl were the clear favourites to win the 4 x 100 metres Relay. The 'dream team' cruised through the first round and the semi-final to face Canada, Jamaica and Italy in the final. Graddy and Brown stormed away and Smith opened up a 3.5 metres lead on the bend while Carl stretched the winning margin to 8 metres as he scorched along the final straight in 8.94 sec. That climatic burst of speed brought Carl his fourth gold medal, thus fulfilling his ambition to repeat Jesse Owens' four victories at the 1936 Berlin Olympics. The US team's winning time of 37.83 sec was the first and only *world* record of the 1984 Games. After the race, in full view of millions watching in the stadium and on world-wide television, the Americans knelt on the track in prayer and gave thanks for their victory.

Asked for his reaction to equalling Owens' achievement, Carl replied: 'To duplicate one of track and field's greatest feats is an honour. Everybody said it couldn't be done. Even I said over a year ago that I didn't think I could do it. But I feel good about it because I worked hard for it. I have many people to thank—my family, my friends, Joe Douglas my manager and Tom Tellez my coach. Carl Lewis is not the only one that did this. There are a lot of people involved. Jesse Owens is still the same man to me as he was before—he is a legend. I'm just a person.'

Early in the 1985 season, Carl continued to turn in good performances. In April, he won the 100 metres in a time of 9.90 sec at the Mount San Antonio College Relays in Walnut, California—3/100th of a second inside the world record of 9.93 sec by Calvin Smith—but not counting as a new record as it was wind-assisted. On May 11, he ran a 9.98 sec 100 metres, the best world performance of 1985.

At the UCLA Meeting in Los Angeles in May, he long jumped a wind assisted 8.77 metres, only 13 centimetres short of Bob Beamon's elusive altitude record. One record he did break on this occasion was George Brown's run of 41 long jump wins between 1950 and 1952. While jumping at Los Angeles, Carl sustained a hamstring injury and was not fully recovered when he competed in the United States Championships at Indianapolis in June. Although he won the Long Jump with a below-form distance of 6.92 metres, in the 100 metres he suffered his first defeat in two years when he came fourth in the semi-final.

Because of his injury, Carl had to delay his much-heralded European tour which was to include the IAAF Mobil Grand Prix meetings. He opened his campaign in Zurich on August 21, but still suffering the effects of the muscle strain, he could only achieve fourth place in the 100 metres and scratched from the 200. Two days later, in West Berlin, he was beaten in the 200 metres by fellow Americans, Baptiste, Smith and Butler. In Cologne, on August 25 he showed better form in the 100 metres, coming second to Marian Woronin of Poland, after making a very slow start. However, in September, Carl won three events in the USA v USSR v Japan match in Tokyo. On the first day he beat Harvey Glance by a metre in the 100 then joined Glance, Kirk Baptise and Calvin Smith in winning the 4 x 100 metres relay. The next day, in wet and cold conditions, Carl won the long jump with a leap of 8.28m. 'It was a good jump for me,' he commented. 'I've only jumped once since April.' Although hampered by injury in 1985, Carl is still reckoned to be the athlete most likely to establish new world records in the long jump and sprints.

In spite of his achievements, Carl's Christian faith is such an important part of his life that he still spends several weeks each year working with 'Lay Witnesses for Christ'. He speaks to youth groups and athletics teams about having a personal relationship with Christ and tells them everyone can have that same relationship. 'We try to show them that, here we are—some of the best athletes in the world—yet

Jesus Christ is first in our lives,' says Carl. 'We want to introduce more people to Christ, because he's the only way. If you don't have a chance to share that way, then you are being cheated. You're not getting the full benefits of life if you are not a Christian.'

Carl lives in a two-storey Victorian style house in Houston. He has a Samoyed dog named Tasha, and a collection of china, crystal and silver brought back from his trips abroad. He has been studying drama for the last two years at the New York actors workshop conducted by Warren Robertson. 'Acting is a nice new challenge,' says Carl. 'It is exciting to do something different like acting, yet something that presents me with a challenge similar to athletic competition.'

Carl recognises that God has given him the gifts which make him one of the world's greatest athletes. 'There's no question that the good Lord has given me a lot of talent, a talent that other people don't have,' he says. 'But it's important that you improve on that talent all the time. Success is about hard work and never giving up.'

Carl also realises that he has a responsibility to use his gift in the service of God. 'I've been given a talent and I've been given a trust, and that trust is speaking for the Lord because I love Him so much. Jesus Christ is number one in my life.' Asked what he considers the best thing about his fame, he replies, 'That I can help others to find the peace of mind that I have through Christ.'

12: 'Fast Freddie'

Freddie Spencer: Double World Motor Cycle Champion

Born 20 December 1961

A newspaper clipping in Freddie Spencer's scrapbook reads: 'Freddie has won 83 of the 90 races he has entered and holds state championships in Texas, Oklahoma, Arkansas, Mississippi and Louisiana.' That was in 1972 and, at the time, Freddie was only *ten* years old. He actually began racing when he was six. In his first mini-bike race he finished last—the chain kept coming off the sprocket on his bike. Freddie says, 'I told dad after that race, that if he still wanted me to do this, we'd have to come up with a better motorcycle.'

Freddie's parents, particularly his father Fred snr., have played an important part in his evolution as a motorcycle racer. His mother, June, says, 'He grew up with it. His father raced, and his brother raced. He'd been going to races since he was six months old. Freddie was determined from the start. He could ride anything he got on.'

Freddie was born in Shreveport, a city in the north-west corner of the state of Louisiana, USA. His parents owned a grocery store and, in addition, his father maintained the family's racing bikes—at one point as many as fifteen.

Following the racing circuit meant long drives in the family van amidst grease, oil and spare parts. Their journeys took them from the crushed clay and limestone dirt oval of the Boot Hill Speedway in Shreveport to Ross Downs in Texas, Lawton Speedway in Oklahoma and Benton Speedbowl in Arkansas. The Spencer family did not relax or take holidays, they went racing instead. As a boy, Freddie spent

166

up to five hours a day practising on a makeshift track around the two acres surrounding his home. The family dedication and effort brought results. When he was eight, Freddie won his first race, on the dirt track at the Louisiana State Fair. It was then that he decided he was going to be a professional motorcycle racer.

Freddie began to win consistently on the dirt track circuit, often beating established riders much older than himself. He was the mini-bike champion of Texas and Oklahoma in 1970 and 1971, and in 1972 added three other state championships. A race report of March 1973, notes that, 'Little Freddie Spencer is only eleven years old, 80 pounds, and four feet eight inches tall, but goes like a mini-Kenny Roberts on the track.'

This report must have thrilled Freddie, as Kenny Roberts was his boyhood hero. 'Whenever I could, I used to go and watch Kenny race on the dirt tracks,' Freddie says. 'Even as a youngster I respected him because he seemed perfect in style and performance. When I was only eleven years old, Kenny was the national champion. He must have been twenty one then, but he seemed far older than me. He was an adult, I was still only a boy.' The age gap between Roberts and himself was so great that the idea of racing against him, let alone beating him, never entered his wildest dreams at that time.

Freddie was baptised in the Summer Glow Baptist Church in Shreveport and went to Sunday School and to church with his family. His was a steady growth in the Christian faith, but at the age of ten, he made a conscious decision to follow Christ. His faith was simple and sincere and, in spite of all the distractions of his busy life, he continued to grow in faith. Freddie spent six years at the Greywood Christian Academy, where he worked hard and enjoyed various sports apart from motor cycle racing. He excelled at basketball, and he was in his school team when it contested the Louisiana State Championship. Freddie, who is now five feet ten inches tall says, 'If I had been a foot taller, perhaps even a little taller, I'd have gone for basketball, maybe professionally'.

When he was twelve, Freddie's career took a momentous turn—he began road racing. On a wet Autumn day in 1974, he took part in his first road race, and, as with his original debut on a mini-bike, came last. Meanwhile, he continued dirt track racing and had his most successful season in 1975. Riding in the 125cc, 250cc and 300cc classes, the thirteen year old won all the 51 races in which he competed.

It was not long before he also began winning class championships in the highly competitive world of WERA* road racing, beating competitors up to ten years older than himself. As in dirt track racing, he had to work his way up from the smaller engined bikes to the more powerful.

During 1976, he took four first places. He also beat the twice American champion, Gary Nixon, in a 250cc road race in Ohio—this was the year when Nixon only narrowly missed becoming World F750 Champion. Freddie was awarded the title, WERA 'Cafe Racer of the Year'.

To obtain maximum experience, Freddie sometimes raced in as many as five classes on one day. On one such day in July 1977, when he was fifteen, he won four classes at a WERA meeting at Lexington, Ohio, and took a second against some of the best professional racers of the day. He repeated this kind of winning performance throughout the season so that by its conclusion, he held four class titles and had enough fans for one of them to start a Freddie Spencer Fan Club. He was nicknamed 'Fast Freddie'—a title he has amply justified.

At sixteen, Freddie was eligible for an AMA* professional licence and he celebrated the start of his professional career with a resounding victory in the 76 mile, 250cc Daytona Novice class race. Gary Von Voorhis, editor

*Western Eastern Road-racing Association.

*American Motorcyclist Association.

of *Cycle News* commented afterwards, 'I knew when I saw him that his was an extraordinary talent whose limits were boundless'. During the year, Freddie teamed up with the renowned American engine tuner, Erv Kanemoto. Apart from a short break in 1981, they have remained together ever since and Freddie feels that linking with Kanemoto was one of the most significant steps in his career. 1978 was the year Freddie won every AMA race in which he finished and took convincingly the title, 'AMA Novice Road Race Champion'.

The following year, Freddie rode Kanemoto's Lightweight Yamaha to take his second AMA title, '250cc Expert Champion, 1979'. He also had two Superbike wins at Daytona on a Kawasaki and coast to coast wins in dirt tracking on a 750cc Harley-Davidson.

At the end of the 1979 season, the big four motorcycle manufacturers, Honda, Kawasaki, Suzuki and Yamaha, each approached Freddie offering him sponsorships. Freddie signed up with Honda to ride the American Superbike class in 1980. However, since at that time, Honda had no competitive Formula One bike, Freddie was also free to ride Kanemoto's 750cc Yamaha.

Although he had already won some Superbike races, Freddie had yet to prove himself on the big bikes. The Daytona 200, America's premier road racing event, held in March, was his opportunity. At eighteen, Freddie had a chance to be the first novice and the youngest rider ever to win the Daytona Classic. At first it seemed as though he would. He charged into the lead, and by the midway point had set a new average speed record, lapped all but seven riders and was a minute ahead of his nearest rival. But on lap 39 of the 52 laps, the Yamaha's crankshaft broke and he was forced to retire.

In his first race after Daytona, at Charlotte, North Carolina, while leading the race, the Yamaha's oil filter came loose and oil poured on Freddie's rear tyre. He crashed at 140 mph, and was fortunate to walk away with only a lacerated knee and a crack to the bridge of his nose.

A month later, Freddie crossed the Atlantic for his first competition outside the United States, the Marlborough Transatlantic Trophy Match Races between the USA and Britain. For the youngster from Shreveport, it was almost beyond belief that he should find himself in the same team as his boyhood hero, Kenny Roberts—now World Champion, and Randy Mamola, another star American rider. In his first two races at Brands Hatch, the eighteen year old stunned everyone by soundly beating Roberts, Barry Sheene, Mamola, Crosby and the rest to win both legs on his 750cc Yamaha. He was second and third at Mallory Park, and a close second to Roberts at Oulton Park. In the second race at Oulton Park, Freddie crashed on the fifth lap, while holding a 100 yard lead. The American team won the series by 72 points. For Freddie, it was an auspicious entry to European racing.

In July, Freddie was back in Europe, in Belgium, for his first Grand Prix. However, the 500cc Yamaha he was riding vibrated so badly on the fast, bumpy Zolder circuit that its petrol tank split, forcing Freddie to retire.

Freddie finished the season a disappointing third for Honda in the US Superbike series, but with his appetite whetted for the European circuit and world level competition. 'I realised the magnitude of Grand Prix racing', he said, 'and I wanted the World Championship.'

It was an ambitious statement of intent from the eighteen year old, and it was therefore a surprise to his fans when he decided to remain in America in 1981 to continue to contest the National Series of dirt track and road races, plus the Superbike series. 'I grew up dirt track racing,' he explains, 'and every young American racer dreams of that Number One plate.' However, the Honda bikes were still in the early development stage and, at the end of the season, it was Eddie Lawson riding for Kawasaki, who took the Superbike series title. Freddie was runner-up; he was also third in the FI championship.

The 1982 season began well in March, at Daytona Beach, with a win in the Superbike road race and, in spite of shedding two rear tyres, a second place in the prestigious 200 mile race. Having failed again to win the coveted Daytona 200 title, Freddie decided to commit himself totally to Grand Prix road racing, joining world champion Marco Lucchinelli and Takazumi Tatayama in the Honda works team.

In his first appearance on the new Honda NS-500 at Buenos Aires in the Argentina Grand Prix, Freddie found himself matched against former world champions Barry Sheene *and* Kenny Roberts. 'Really the Argentina was the first proper race I had with Kenny', Freddie recalls. 'It was a problem for me to overcome—the fact that I had such a great respect for his riding ability. Of course, for me, he was *the* man to try and beat.' To everyone's astonishment, the young newcomer to grand prix racing took the lead in the early stages of the gruelling race and finished an impressive third behind Roberts and Sheene, and well ahead of his distinguished team mate, Lucchinelli, the defending world champion.

Freddie's first continental Grand Prix, at the Salzbur-gring, Austria, came to an abrupt end when the Honda's crankshaft broke as he was beginning to move up on the leaders. After setting the fastest lap time at the next Grand Prix in Jarama, Spain, an ignition coil vibrated loose as Freddie led the race and once again he had to retire. A week later, the Honda team's fortunes took a turn for the better. Franco Uncino, the eventual World Champion, won on his home track at Monza, Italy, and Freddie came second. It was his best Grand Prix result to date and the Press hailed him as an up-and-coming star.

Success can bring with it the mental stress of high expectations. However, the combination of Freddie's temperament and his deep Christian faith enable him to remain calm under pressure. He prays before each race, and his trust in God gives him a sense of tranquility that manifests itself before and during a big race. 'The way I've looked at it all these years I've been racing,' he says, 'is I can only do my best. The only pressure I feel is what I put on myself. I don't get any more nervous five minutes before a race than I do five or six hours before one.'

From Italy the teams moved to Holland for the Dutch Grand Prix at Assen. The race was marred by a torrential downpour and Freddie was one of four riders who skidded and fell. The race was stopped, and later re-started, but without Freddie, who was forced to withdraw due to a technical infringement involved with the rebuilding of his damaged machine in the interval between the two legs of the race.

A week later, on the 4th of July, at the Francorchamps circuit at Spa, Belgium, Freddie achieved his first Grand Prix win. He also gave Honda their first Grand Prix victory in fifteen years, set a new track record and, at twenty, became the youngest-ever Grand Prix winner. A year later, in an interview for the magazine, *Motorcycle Racing*, Freddie reflected on that epic victory. 'When I won in Belgium last year it was a big moment in my career. But I suppose in the back of my mind was the fact that I had actually won a race against my childhood hero. If I could beat *him* I must have got somewhere in this racing game.' Beating Kenny Roberts in no way diminished the admiration and respect Freddie felt for him. He said, 'I do consider him still to be the best rider around and certainly the best to race against'.

In the next Grand Prix, in Yugoslavia, Freddie overcame minor technical problems for a fourth place. Two weeks later he returned to Silverstone and registered a very creditable second in the British Grand Prix. He finished behind Uncini, who clinched the world title when Roberts, his main rival, had a spill on the first lap. Freddie now had a chance of being runner-up in the championship if he could do well in the remaining schedule of races. His hopes were dashed, however, when he failed to finish in the Swedish Grand Prix, but rose again when, a month later, he took first place in the San Marino Grand Prix in Italy. Once more he was a serious contender for second place in the world standings.

The final race was on the fast Hockenheimring, in West Germany. Freddie rode brilliantly and, towards the end of the race, was cruising to what appeared to be a certain win. With half a lap to go, he had what he thought was a comfortable lead over the second and third place riders. With only two bends left before the chequered flag, he braked for the penultimate curve. Franco Uncini braked late, collided with Freddie and sent him flying across the tarmac. Freddie was rushed to hospital with a broken collarbone, while the second place rider went on to win. Without gaining points in the final round, Freddie slipped to third place in the world rankings for 1982. Nonetheless, to come third was an outstanding feat for his first full Grand Prix season and *Motor Cycle News* was justified in naming him as the 'Rider of the Year'.

As the 1983 season began, Kenny Roberts, three times world 500cc champion was ready to do battle for a fourth world title before retiring. It was Freddie Spencer, ten years his junior, whom he saw as his chief rival. Interviewed by John Brown of *Motorcycle Racing*, Kenny said, 'He was good last year in his first GP season but his equipment was not staying together. He is a very talented rider, the best I have ever raced with as far as ability to ride a motorcycle is concerned. If you want a rival who's for a fight all the way then Freddie just has to fill the spot. Any time you have as much talent as Freddie and as good machinery as he's got this year, you have a winning combination.'

The former world champion's assessment proved correct. His twenty year old rival staked his claim to the championship with a runaway win in the opening Grand Prix at Kyalami, South Africa on March 19.

At the French Grand Prix at Le Mans, Roberts was the fastest qualifier, but in the race it was Freddie's quick-starting Honda that took the lead. Roberts passed Freddie on the seventh lap, but seven laps later he was slowed with a cracked exhaust muffler. Freddie flashed by to win and set up a new lap record.

The following week, in the Italian Grand Prix, Freddie

led an unprecedented finish, with Americans taking the top three places: Spencer, Mamola, Lawson. Roberts, who would have made it a US quartet, ran out of fuel on the last lap and lost precious championship points.

Although the thumb-shaped Hockenheim course appeared to favour the horsepower of the Yamahas in the West German Grand Prix on May 8, Freddie on the Honda, soon went ahead. 'I had a five second lead,' says Freddie, 'when I realised the number two-underneath-exhaust was beginning to go. I knew then that I just had to try to keep going and score as many points as possible.' As Freddie slowed down, Roberts sped by and gradually Freddie dropped back to fourth. He was about to be overtaken by a group of five riders including Lawson and Mamola, when a rainstorm deluged the track. The race was red-flagged to a premature conclusion and Freddie kept his fourth place. He now had a lead of 53 points to Roberts' 35 points in the World Championship.

In the fifth race of the season, the Spanish Grand Prix at Madrid, the 65,000–strong crowd witnessed some breathtaking racing by Freddie and Kenny Roberts. The British rider, Ron Haslam, took an early lead. Freddie then went to the front until overtaken by Roberts, who raced to a fifty-metre lead. In a dazzling display of knee-to-the-ground riding, Freddie gradually overhauled the Yamaha and passing Roberts four laps from the end, went on to win the race by some three metres. At the finish, Freddie was so exhausted he could hardly climb off his bike. 'I knew Kenny wouldn't give up,' he said, 'that was the hardest race of my life.'

By the half-way stage in the twelve race season, Freddie had amassed a lead of 21 championship points. But his run of victories was broken in the Austrian Grand Prix when his engine expired on the twelfth lap. Roberts had his easiest win of the year, with Lawson second and Mamola third. Freddie was now only six points ahead and the final result was wide open again.

Two weeks later, at Rijeka in Yugoslavia, Freddie was

the fastest qualifier and rode a superb race to finish ahead of Mamola and Lawson. Roberts had trouble starting his Yamaha and watched the field disappear round the first bend before he got away, but after an inspired display of riding through the pack, came in fourth to pick up championship points.

As they went into the Dutch Grand Prix at Assen, Freddie led Roberts by 83 points to 70. Roberts was on pole position but again his bike would not start. Freddie went off into the lead only to slow down with frame-flex problems caused by the wrong choice of tyres. First Roberts, then team-mate Katayama, surged past and Freddie did well to nurse his badly-handling motorcycle into third place.

The next week, the contest was continued at Spa in the Belgium Grand Prix. Starting as fastest qualifier, Freddie shot into the lead, but again had tyre trouble, this time with his front tyre. On the thirteenth lap Roberts swept past and surged round the remaining seven laps to win, with Freddie runner-up and now only five points ahead in the rankings.

The British Grand Prix at Silverstone was crucial for both the main contenders for the world title. On the fifth lap, a horrific accident in the rain claimed the lives of two riders and the race was brought to a halt. Under international regulations, the first five laps were scored as a first leg, in which Roberts was placed first and Freddie second. The second leg, after the re-start, consisted of twenty-three laps, and Roberts again took the lead and held it while the battle raged for the next three places. Freddie with a piston ring stuck, could only manage fourth, but when the aggregate times were calculated he scraped into second place by nine-hundreths of a second, with Mamola and Lawson third and fourth. Roberts' victory was just what he needed to keep his hopes alive for a fourth World Championship. Freddie was now only two points ahead of his older and more experienced rival.

The penultimate race of the championship, the Swedish

Grand Prix at Anderstorp on August 7, was a critical race for the two leading contenders. Freddie led for the first six laps before giving way to Roberts. During the last ten laps they battled it out wheel to wheel, with Roberts holding a slight advantage down to the last lap. Freddie then made a controversial move. Going into the final corner, a downhill 90–degree right-hander leading to the finishing line, Roberts failed to protect the inside line of the corner. Freddie braked very late, and pulled up beside Roberts forcing him off the outside of the track. Freddie, barely off the track, accelerated back on to the tarmac and snatched the win by 0.16 seconds over the irate Roberts. Afterwards Freddie apologised to Roberts but maintained that it was a fair manoeuvre.

Freddie's lead for the title was now a tentative five points. The final race of the season, the Swedish Grand Prix at Imola, would decide the championship. Freddie knew the championship was his if he just finished second to Roberts, but he could not afford to let anyone finish between him and his rival. In his familiar red, white and blue leathers, Freddie made a fast start on the Honda and led until the eighth lap when the red-clad Roberts, on his red and white Yamaha went to the front. In his effort to snatch the lead, Roberts set up a new lap record. Freddie, riding a tactical race, was content to stay behind him, but made sure he kept well ahead of Lawson and the other riders. Although Roberts took the chequered flag by 1.23 seconds, Freddie's second place was good enough to give him the World Championship with 144 points to Roberts' 142; third place went to Mamola with 89 points. Having beaten his boyhood hero, twenty-one year old 'Fast Freddie' was the youngest ever holder of the blue riband of motorcycling and Honda's first 500cc world champion.

Kenny Roberts retired from Grand Prix without his fourth world title and Freddie started the 1984 season hopeful of a second World Championship ahead of his main rivals, fellow Americans Randy Mamola and Eddie Lawson, and the Frenchman, Raymond Roche. When Freddie was actually riding, he was all but unbeatable. Out of the eight races he contested, he won five and was second in another. But having missed five Grand Prix, through various injuries he had no hope of retaining his World Championship title and had to be content with fourth place, with 87 points. The Californian, Eddie Lawson, was the eventual winner with 142 points, his compatriot Mamola second with 111 and Roche third, scoring 99 points.

Freddie's primary objective for the 1985 season was to regain the World 500cc Championship. Honda also decided to enter him in the 250cc class in the hope of gaining the double championship—a feat never before accomplished by either rider or manufacturer.

Freddie began his racing year at Daytona in March, using the Formula One race and the 250cc race—both of which he won—to sharpen his riding skills ready for the first Grand Prix in South Africa two weeks later. At Kyalami, Freddie won the 28 lap 250cc race, then swopped Hondas for the 500cc event. Although he had demolished the lap record in practice, in the race itself, it was the new world champion who fought magnificently to beat Freddie by five seconds, thus foiling his first attempt at a double victory.

Two hours before the Spanish Grand Prix in Jarama on May 5, Freddie took a high-speed tumble. It happened when the front wheel of his Honda slid away on a fast right hand bend during the final pre-race test session. Fast work by his mechanics repaired the damaged bike in time for the start. Although in considerable pain from cuts and bruises on his right arm, Freddie rode a heroic race to withstand Lawson's strong challenge; his win levelled the points in the Championship. Wisely, he withdrew from the 250cc event which took place immediately after the longer race.

Freddie was the favourite for a double victory in the West German Grand Prix on May 19. He started off well in the 500cc event, forging to the front at the end of the first lap in wet, treacherous conditions. At half-distance he looked unbeatable but then the Honda V4's rear tyre started to break up and he finished in second place, twelve seconds behind the Frenchman, Christian Sarron. 'Pieces of rubber were flying off, so I suppose I was lucky to finish at all,' said Freddie afterwards. In the 250cc class, he was second once more, being beaten by Martin Wimmer of West Germany. At the end of the day, Freddie topped the 500cc standings with 30 points and lay third in the 250cc class.

The following week at Mugello, Italy, Freddie took the lead on the second lap of the 500cc event and cruised to an easy victory, 9.24 sec ahead of the defending champion. He stepped straight from his V4 Honda to the smaller, twin cylinder machine and fought his way through the 250cc field to snatch the lead just five laps from the flag, beating the reigning champion Carlos Lavado by 2.79 sec. In so doing he became the first man for nine years to win two World Championship races in one Grand Prix meeting. Afterwards Freddie declared, 'This is the greatest day of my life. Now I want to be the first ever double world champion.' He was already on his way—the victories at Mugello gave him an overall lead in both classes.

A week later, Freddie edged a step closer to achieving his ambition with another double in the Austrian Grand Prix at the Salzburgring. He steered his 250cc Honda across the line ahead of Anton Mang of Germany to record his first success of the day. Then he claimed victory in the 500cc event on aggregate times when heavy rain interrupted the 30 lap race just after the half-way stage. Lawson was runner up, only 0.03 sec behind. After five rounds of the Championship, Freddie now led the 500cc standings with 69 points, ten clear of Lawson, and led the 250cc class with 59 points, nine more than Mang.

In the Yugoslavian Grand Prix at Rijeka, Freddie increased his lead in the 250cc championship with a runaway victory from Yamaha's title defender, Lavado. However, Lawson narrowed the gap in his battle to retain the World title with a sensational victory in the 500cc race. On the fourth lap Freddie ran wide in an all-out effort to take the lead from team-mate Randy Mamola and, at over 100 mph, smashed his right leg into a trackside straw bale.

Wrestling with his heavy machine, Freddie just managed to avoid crashing and, in spite of excruciating pain, struggled on for the remaining twenty-nine laps. Mamola passed him again only to crash with nine laps to go when one of his wheels broke away. Lawson came through to win and Freddie crossed the line in a heroic second place and toppled from his bike in a state of collapse. He was rushed off for medical treatment to a badly torn thigh muscle while Lawson mounted the victor's rostrum. Freddie, who admitted his accident was due to an error of judgement said, 'I just don't know how I finished the race. At one time, I thought I was going to pass out. I just hope I'll be fit for the Dutch TT in two weeks' time.' The defeat cut Freddie's lead to seven points at the half-way stage in the twelve-round series.

Freddie did recover sufficiently to contest the Dutch TT at Assen and increased his lead in the 250cc championship with a clear-cut victory. However, on the opening lap of the 500cc race the rain caused the first of many falls. Christian Sarron was blinded by spray as he came out of a bend and careered off the track, taking Freddie with him. Both escaped unhurt but were unable to restart. Lawson failed to capitalise when he, too, crashed on the treacherous surface at the half-way stage, leaving Mamola to win his first Grand Prix of the season.

However, the following week, Freddie dominated the Belgian Grand Prix at Francorchamps, winning both the 250cc and 500cc events at record-breaking speeds. In the 250cc event he led from start to finish of the 16–lap race, to beat Carlos Lavado by almost 13 seconds and open up a massive class championship lead of 34 points over Anton Mang. Freddie then switched to his V4 Honda for the 500cc race, went to the front from the outset and soon built up a commanding lead on the beautiful four mile circuit that winds through the Ardennes forest. Motor-Cycling correspondent George Turnbull wrote, 'It is some time since the Belgian enthusiasts have been treated twice in an afternoon to such a display of racing artistry by one man, and the 120,000 crowd rose to the American.'

At Le Mans, on July 21, Freddie scored yet another double in the French Grand Prix. Lawson made a terrible start on his Yamaha and Freddie was hotly pursued by Wayne Gardner, the promising young Australian rider, and Raymond Roche who was cheered on by his home crowd. Unfortunately for Gardner, the rear tyre of his Honda began to break up as he went into the lead and forced his retirement on the twelfth lap. Christian Sarron took up the challenge, but as he pulled alongside Freddie on a very tight corner, the Frenchman braked too hard and crashed, leaving Freddie out on his own to win 16 seconds ahead of Roche, with Mamola third. Freddie went on to register his fourth 'double'. It was his sixth consecutive win in the 250cc event and he finished 10 seconds in front of Anton Mang. Freddie now had a 27 point lead over Mang in the 250cc World Championship—the title could be his on the next round.

Much was at stake when Freddie arrived at Silverstone for the British Grand Prix. Silverstone is the fastest of the championship circuits and, during practice, Freddie was asked if that worried him. 'Speed is not the fear,' he replied, 'lapping at 180mph does not mean all that much, but how the tyres will behave does cause some worry.' Questioned about his religious beliefs, he said, 'I will pray on Sunday as I do every day. Not for safe delivery, not for any special favours, but simply that I will do myself justice . . . that I will perform to the very best of my ability.' 'Is the money important?' he was asked. 'What I want to be known for is the way I ride a bike,' Freddie replied, 'the way I hope everyone who competes against me tries their hardest to be better . . . the way we shake hands at the beginning and say "Good Luck". And the way we shake hands at the end and say: "Well done".'

Race day dawned with pouring rain and high winds sweeping the Northamptonshire circuit. On a very slippery track, in blinding spray, Freddie took no chances in the

250cc event, and rode a cautious race, content to finish fourth—knowing that the result was sufficient to give him the World Championship. Then, he climbed straight on to his 500cc V4 bike, pausing only to comment, 'These are the worst conditions I've ever raced in.'

Freddie went into the lead before the first bend and, in spite of the atrocious conditions, soon opened up an 18 second gap on his nearest rivals. Described by one correspondent as 'a projectile ahead of a cloud of spray', Freddie powered his way through the slower riders to lap all but the first five. By the later stages of the race, Eddie Lawson had come through to second place after a slow start and a long battle with third-placed Sarron. Freddie, however, had such a commanding lead that he was able to ease up over the last few laps, although taking care to maintain at least an 8–second 'cushion' between himself and Lawson. With two rounds left in the 500cc Championship, Freddie was now 21 points ahead of the 1984 champion. As for the 250cc Championship, without having to compete in the remaining two races, the title was already his.

A week after winning the world 250cc championship, Freddie made motor-cycling history when he won his second 500cc crown with a runaway victory in the Swedish TT. Freddie needed only to finish third to take the title but he was not interested in a 'safe' result. Leading the race from the second lap, he finished 22.8 clear of Eddie Lawson, the deposed champion. 'I wanted to win the championship by winning the race,' Freddie explained, 'and I'm pleased that's the way it went.'

So Freddie became the first man to win both titles in one year. 'It's a dream come true for me,' said Honda's star rider, 'and it's only just starting to sink in that I've achieved something that's never been done before.' He achieved his unique double with 14 wins, four seconds, one fourth and a ninth place. Barry Sheene, 500cc world champion in 1976–7, says of Freddie, 'He is simply the best motor cycle racer the world has seen. He's better than Roberts and better than anyone I have ever raced against. I don't know what it is that makes him special, but special he certainly is.'

Looking to the future, although Freddie is unlikely to contest the 250cc championship, he expects to defend his 500cc title. 'I'll be back,' he says, 'and I'll go on giving 100 per cent.' He hints, however, that he may eventually switch from two wheels to four, 'I won't be racing motorcycles into my late twenties, that's for sure,' says the 23–year old champion. 'I've had some opportunities to make the change to cars and, if I eventually do, I guess I'll have to practice somewhere in secret!'

Freddie is a home-loving person and, when possible in between races, he likes to return to the peace and security of his house in Shreveport. While at home he enjoys golf, tennis, trail-riding and riding his wet-bike on a nearby lake. He still has a passion for basketball, both playing for fun and as a spectator at major league games.

To handle the business affairs that have developed from his success as a sportsman, Freddie Spencer Racing Inc. was formed some years ago with its head office in Shreveport. Freddie is well aware of the responsibility his fame has brought and is committed to making a contribution to the sport that means so much to him. Already he has helped to change the bad image of motorcyclists that many people have. As one journalist said, 'He is the kind of guy you hope your daughter will bring home one day'. Freddie knows how sportsmen and women can influence the young and says, 'I get letters from kids every day and I don't want to come across as a bad example to them.'

Religion is a very personal experience to Freddie and yet he does not hide the fact that he is a Christian, and seeks to express his convictions in his way of life. A member of his staff says, 'Freddie just lives his faith, every day of his life he is consistently a Christian. He is a very kind hearted person who always sees the best in everybody and never says an unkind word about anyone. He does not smoke or drink and his way of life is something of an exception in the racing world. To live the kind of life he does, to travel

182

the world, to become such a success and yet to remain unchanged, is a great demonstration of the deep sincerity of his Christianity.'

Community service is one way in which Freddie's faith finds expression. Since before his first World Championship, he has sponsored a softball team from his Shreveport Honda dealership, playing for it when he is available. He also sponsors a bicycle Motorcross team and dirt track car racing. In conjunction with two banks and the local branch of the American Diabetes Association, he has sponsored an Autumn 'Walk for Diabetes' from which the money raised has benefitted children's diabetes camps, diabetes research and education. Freddie's other recent projects have included help for the Northwest Louisiana Lion's Eye Bank and Shreveport Eye Research Foundation. Whenever a friend or charitable organisation calls for assistance, he is ready to give time, energy and funds, although he does so unobtrusively and without seeking any public recognition.

His agent says of him, 'Though he has the self-confidence which comes with success, plus the steel core of ambition that marks any true champion, Freddie Spencer is, in fact, a modest young man. He is always ready to acknowledge the achievements of his rivals and to overlook their shortcomings'. His instant smile, athletic build and charm make him much sought after for television; he has appeared on nationally syndicated shows to discuss his racing career, his outside interests and his religious beliefs. As Yale Youngblood of *Time Sports* says, 'He comes across in interviews just as his friends and family say he does in everyday life—a personable, sincere, extremely hard-working and courteous young man'.

Dennis McKay, one of Honda's executives, believes the company could not have found a better rider to sponsor. 'Freddie,' he says, 'is just a great, well-rounded person, the perfect representative for our company. Our slogan is: "You meet the nicest people on a Honda". Well, we have proved that's true with Freddie.'

Michael Scott, motorcycling correspondent of *The Times*,

says, 'the world champion is a devout man in a profane setting' who lives 'life in the fast lane but *keeps on the right track*.'

13: Getting Organised

'Christians in Sport' and Chaplains to Sport

For some years there have existed in the USA organisations to promote Christianity among sportsmen and women, notably the Fellowship of Christian Athletes and Pro Athletes Outreach. In April 1975, a small group of enthusiasts in Britain formed themselves into a fellowship with a similar purpose in mind. They called themselves 'Christians in Sport' (CIS) and their aim was to meet and share their common concern for the spiritual needs of sport and athletics in Britain.

In June 1976, the first 'Annual CIS Dinner' was held in London to bring together as many Christians as possible among those competing or involved in British sports. The enthusiasm generated by that inaugural meeting led to a demand for a more formal structure for the fellowship to enable it to extend its influence into the many varied areas of sports. It was decided that Christians engaged in sport should take on the responsibility for discovering other Christians in their particular sport and for establishing contact with them, where this was possible.

Over the last few years, CIS has grown steadily in many ways. There are now a thousand names on the list of associates and supporters. Active groups meeting regularly exist in London, Lancashire and Torquay. It is hoped to develop a country-wide network and plans are in progress for other groups in the North and Midlands. In the universities and colleges there is a growing interest among sports people in the work of CIS, and already groups have been established at Oxford, Cambridge, Durham, Bristol and Bedford, with others in prospect elsewhere.

Sportsmen's Dinners are still an important means of outreach by CIS. They are now organised on a regional basis with annual dinners being held in London, the North West and South West. The dinners are aimed particularly at professional sportspeople who come as guests of the organisers. After the meal there is usually a singer and one or two speakers from the world of sport who will testify to the importance of Jesus Christ in their lives. John Motson and Gerald Williams, well known television sports commentators, have also been used to interview men and women from a variety of sports—professional and amateur.

CIS has also encouraged the appointment of local ministers to serve as chaplains to professional sports clubs. John Boyers, a Baptist minister in Watford, speaks about this aspect of the work: 'In the United States all the professional basketball and grid-iron football clubs have a chaplain. At present about 15 English soccer teams have chaplains. Christians in Sport would like to have a chaplain appointed to every professional football club in the UK. The role of the chaplain is essentially to get alongside the players in a football (or other) club, to befriend them, to be available if they want help or advice. Since 1977 I have been privileged to be a kind of chaplain to Watford FC. Initially I approached the club and made some suggestions as to how the idea of appointing a chaplain could be of assistance to the club. I felt that I could help in situations of illness, beareavement and personal problems. Over the years my involvement in the club has been in a variety of ways. Often I have tried to train with the team one day a week in order to maintain contact with the players. If a player is injured and has to go into hospital, I try to visit him and to encourage him as he seeks to regain fitness and his place in the team. When a new player joins the club I seek to help him to settle into the area. In these and other ways I have tried to be of service to players and to the club. The pressures on the

186

modern professional sportsman are immense. Many clubs go to great lengths to ensure the physical well-being of their players but spiritually they are on their own. A chaplain can provide a listening ear, a caring concern. He is neutral, confidential. He has no axe to grind. He does not represent the club or the manager but is there for no other reason than that he cares.'

In the early years, CIS was nurtured and developed under the wing of Deo Gloria Outreach, a Trust which had provided them with office space, staff and funds. By the summer of 1980, however, it was felt that the time had come for CIS to become an independent Trust in its own right. In consequence, it became a registered charity with its own full time and part time staff. The Deeds of the Trust state that 'Christians in Sport' exists:

(i)   To proclaim the Christian message of salvation to sports people and others involved in various aspects of sport.

(ii) To provide Christian teaching for, and to strengthen the faith of, Christians already involved in sport.

(iii) To help and encourage Christians in sport to share their faith with other people in sport and in society generally.

(iv) To help and encourage Christians in sport to show their faith by relieving poverty, advancing education and providing recreational facilities for those in need.

'To-day,' say the promoters of CIS 'sport has become a religion for vast masses who are virtually deaf to any kind of challenge from other sources. All around the world top class sports people enjoy the adulation of millions of fans. They are in a unique position to influence the world for Christ. They must be reached with the Gospel of Christ's saving love.'

On 1 September 1984, the Revd Andrew Wingfield Digby was appointed the first 'Christians in Sport' National Director. Andrew gained four cricket blues at Oxford and has subsequently played club cricket for Cockfosters and for Dorset in the Minor Counties. CIS is a church based organisation and Andrew is attached to St Aldate's, Oxford.

A 30–minute Video Film has been produced by CIS and is available on request. The film is introduced by Gerald Williams and features sports action and interviews with some well known Christian personalities.

Further details about CIS may be obtained from 'Christians in Sport', PO Box 93, Oxford, OX1 1QX.

A Further View on Chaplaincy

Before CIS was founded, a Methodist minister, the Revd John Jackson was already acting as Chaplain to Leeds United Football Club. He describes his experience in an article that first appeared in the Methodist Church Home Mission Report, 1984.

'Early in 1962 our church at Harehills Lane arranged a sportsmen's service at which one of the speakers was the General Manager of Leeds United, the late Mr Cyril Williamson. I met Mr Williamson prior to the service and suggested to him that Leeds United might find a chaplain useful. The word 'surprise' would not adequately cover his reaction to my suggestion. However, we did discuss the matter and he became quite interested and invited me to write to him so that the suggestion might be discussed by the directors. After a matter of weeks I received a letter indicating that the directors had appointed me club chaplain (March 1962).

It was arranged for me to meet Don Revie, the team manager, and his coaching staff. As we discussed the work, I discovered that here, as with the directors, they were giving me an open door to share with them in the work of the club. I met all the senior players and was invited to give a talk to the juniors. The chief thing in relating my work to the juniors was that I was asked to concentrate on 'life in the big city' and the temptations they would have to face. From this the pattern for the future emerged. I was to concentrate on the juniors and their character-building

188

and then to mix freely with seniors, coaching staff, administrative staff, cleaners, laundry workers and ground staff. I was given the freedom of the ground to talk to anyone employed by the club. We arranged that the visits should be weekly on a Thursday morning, as far as possible with a monthly visit for regular talks and discussions with the juniors. It was also agreed that should any player or member of the staff require an interview, a separate time would be arranged either at the ground or at our home.

Successive meetings with the juniors revealed that they often felt lonely away from home and needed someone to talk to outside the paid staff. They took the opportunity of talking to me about all sorts of matters related to their homes and families. They came frequently to our home, many of them joined in the activities of the youth club at the church and occasionally on a Sunday evening one or two could be seen on the back seat at worship. In addition I continued to meet the senior players each week either before or after training, or even both times. In general I was received politely but it seemed difficult to make the same breakthrough as with the juniors.

After I had been going to the club for some months I received a phone call from the Assistant Manager informing me that our club Captain and his wife had lost their young baby. They were both glad to see me, but surprised as they were both regular worshippers at the Anglican Church. They came to understand that as club chaplain, all players and staff were important to me irrespective of their denominations. We prayed together and I left—just a normal visit to a bereaved family.

The next day I went on my weekly visit to the club and on entering the First Team dressing room, I was amazed to hear different voices calling me by name and greeting me with some enthusiasm. I was invited to join them in their after-training cup of tea, and someone said, 'You went to see Fred yesterday—why, he's not one of yours is he?' The moment of breakthrough had come—I was able at last to grasp the opportunity of explaining that denominational barriers meant nothing here and that I was there to serve all of them, by serving my Lord. From then on, the senior professionals, along with the rest of the players, coaches, office and laundry staff, accepted me for what I was—their friend and chaplain.

The door was now open for me and I was led, then as now, to ensure that I was available for a chat. It is still amazing what does arise through casual conversation. Matters and problems which are very personal can lead easily to matters relating to God and faith. Indeed, many and varied have been the problems and conversations over the last 21 years. We have gone through difficult days and of course a long period of happy days at the club, and it has been more and more obvious to me that I must be available. In this connection I am grateful for the help that our church and circuit gave me. They did everything possible to ensure that when I was needed at the club I could be there.

The talks with the juniors still go on every month, and private interviews when necessary for anyone. A casual conversation can still be used by Christ to open doors. Without sounding pious in any way, let me add that I do not go to the ground to take Christ there since I remember that he is there before me. I just go in case he needs an errand boy.

I end with the thought—why do I go? Simply because I believe Christ has sent me. Our task is to go wherever people will receive us, in Christ's name.'

Postscript

'I am sure our basic needs are the same. This is why I recommend Jesus Christ as the only one who can answer your needs and give you "The peace of God that passes all understanding".'

Gary Player